Jim! Thanks for your friendship & Guidance!

THE NEW CONSERVATIVE PARADIGM

THOMAS G DEL BECCARO

THE NEW CONSERVATIVE PARADIGM

ADVANCE PRAISE FOR
THE NEW
CONSERVATIVE PARADIGM

MONA CHAREN, syndicated columnist and Author of *Useful Idiots: How Liberals Got It Wrong in the Cold War and Still Blame America First,* offered the following assessment: *"Well at least someone in the Republican Party is thinking strategically. **Not since Newt Gingrich in the 90s has a Republican activist so clearly analyzed what has gone right and wrong for the party and the conservative movement.**"*

LEW UHLER, President and founder, **along with Milton Friedman**, of the National Tax Limitation Committee, noted: *"**In a beautifully written book, Del Beccaro at once lets readers know the power of economic freedom** and the dangers facing Republicans in the years to come if they don't heed the lessons of **The New Conservative Paradigm.**"*

Author **JACK CASHILL**, *First Strike: TWA Flight 800 and the Attack on America* and *Ron Brown's Body: How One Man's Death Saved the Clinton Presidency and Hillary's Future*, opined on the character of Del Beccaro's *New Conservative Paradigm*: **"The Roman poet Horace would have admired Tom Del Beccaro's *The New Conservative Paradigm*. Ronald Reagan embodied the principle in his person and Del Beccaro captures it in print."**

All statements, analysis, the citation of facts and opinions expressed are solely those of the author and do not reflect the official position of the Publisher, any political party, campaign committee or candidate. Nothing in the contents should be construed as asserting or implying endorsement or authentication of author's views by any political party, campaign committee or candidate. This book is for entertainment purposes only.

THE NEW CONSERVATIVE PARADIGM. Copyright © Thomas G. Del Beccaro. No part of this book may be reproduced in any manner whatsoever without written permission from the Publisher, TMK Books, with the exception of brief quotations embodied in critical articles and reviews. Please purchase only authorized editions and do not participate in or encourage electronic piracy of copyrighted materials.

Cover photograph: Copyright © Thomas G. Del Beccaro

ISBN: 978-0-9801142-0-1
Library of Congress Control Number: 2007939924

Published by TMK Books.
http://www.tmkbooks.net
86 SW Century Drive, Suite 151, Bend, OR 97702 USA

To my Mother for all of her courage and love

To my Father who introduced me to politics, and

To my daughter ~ because everything I do, I do it for you

TABLE OF CONTENTS

- I FOREWARD BY JACK CASHILL
- II INTRODUCTION SILENT NO MORE
- III SOMETHING HAS CHANGED
- IV THE SOUL OF A "ME TOO" PARTY
- V HOPE MATTERS
- VI REAGAN ACHIEVES OUR HEROIC DREAMS
- VII THE THREE PILLARS
- VIII BUSH 41 AND CLINTON LOST YEARS OF OPPORTUNITY
- IX STRENGTHENING THE PARADIGM
- X REPUBLICANS RETURN CLINTON'S FAVOR
- XI THE LESSONS WE SHOULD HAVE LEARNED
- XII LESSONS IN ACTION
- XIII FINAL THOUGHTS AND HOPES
- XIV PUBLISHER'S NOTE

Foreword
By Jack Cashill

It just so happened that after reading a draft of Tom Del Beccaro's *The New Conservative Paradigm*, I had a one-on-one meeting with a candidate for Congress. A sharp guy with a great reputation and good conservative instincts, this state legislator will have an excellent shot at unseating a five-term, Democratic incumbent.

What this candidate lacked, however, at least at this early stage of his campaign, was what the elder George Bush might have called that "vision thing."

Immediately after our meeting, I emailed him a draft of *The New Conservative Paradigm*. "Read this, please," I urged. As I explained, I have not seen anywhere a more lucid blueprint for helping America—in Ronald Reagan's words—to "begin again." My candidate read it and reacted as positively as I did. Let us hope it carries him to victory in 2008.

The Roman poet Horace would have admired Del Beccaro's book as well. It is one of those rare political books that embodies his guiding aesthetic, *simplex munditiis*, or, in English, "elegant simplicity."

President Ronald Reagan embodied in person the aesthetic that Del Beccaro captures in print. As Del Beccaro makes clear, the political philosophy that guided Reagan was so streamlined by logic and so seasoned by experience that his opponents mistook its simple elegance for mere simplicity. History has proved them wrong and in spades.

Understandably, the spirit of President Reagan permeates the book, not just Reagan the ideologue, nor Reagan the optimist, but Reagan the leader.

The Democrats once had leaders. And Del Beccaro does not shy from giving John F. Kennedy credit where it is due. Like Reagan, Kennedy honored the three essentials of the new paradigm: pro-growth policies and reforms, specifically a belief in tax cuts; a belief in America and her defenses, and a respect for American traditions and values.

The Democrats lost their way during the presidency of Lyndon Johnson. While Johnson championed tax increases to "pay for" his wars on poverty and on Vietnamese Communists, his rebellious Democratic opposition championed poverty and the North Vietnamese. For a variety of reasons, none of them good, Democrats collectively abandoned their faith in America. They have not gotten it back.

As night follows day, the Democrats abandoned their faith in the American dream as well. Not since JFK have they had a national leader willing to actually lead and to inspire. Instead, they have settled for managers and not very competent ones at that. For both Jimmy Carter and Bill Clinton every issue had to be haggled over and every policy hacked out. There was no guiding logic to their plans and no respect shown for the intelligence of their constituents.

The 1432-page health care blueprint concocted by Hillary Clinton's 511-person secret task force in 1993 perfectly captured the condescension and clumsy incoherence of contemporary Democratic politics. Happily, the American people rejected stage management by the Clintons for what Del Beccaro nicely describes as "the theater of the possible."

Unfortunately, despite some shining moments, Republican leadership has all too often eschewed the possible for the seemingly safe. This strategy, alas, led to the loss of both houses of Congress in 2006, and Del Beccaro was not the least surprised.

What frustrates him and other Republicans as well is that the model for good leadership still resonates in our memory. What distinguishes Del Beccaro from those other Republicans is that he has converted that frustration into a lively, lucid prescription for positive and permanent change.

To make his case, Del Beccaro uses a deft mix of statistics, anecdotes, and historical data. His analysis is fresh, bright, and straightforward. There is nothing weary or wonkish about it. He reminds Republicans of just how simple and logical is the potential Republican path to success.

I just hope my candidate and a thousand others will follow it.

SILENT NO MORE

"To sin by silence when they should protest makes cowards of men."
Ella Wilcox, American Poet

18 THE NEW CONSERVATIVE PARADIGM

Who will win the next Presidential election? Which Party will control Congress? Will it simply be the Party that is ahead now? Or is there a winning paradigm for successful parties?

The New Conservative Paradigm contends there is more reason than rhyme to winning, a paradigm if you will – and so let our story begin.

Starting in 1980, Republicans began to reverse years of Congressional futility and then began move into the lead nationally. They did so because of the leadership of Ronald Reagan and his forging of a new political paradigm. With the election of George W. Bush, in the year 2000, along with a Republican Congress, the Republicans lead was apparent for all to see. Just six years later, however, they abandoned a key part of the new conservative paradigm and visibly lost a good part of that lead in the 2006 Congressional elections.

It may not be entirely clear how the Republicans got ahead prior to 2006. Perhaps even less obvious is why, during 2005 and 2006, the Republican leaders chose to give up that lead. As we move toward the 2008 elections, and the troublesome decade ahead, Republicans simply must come to an understanding as to how Reagan put us ahead and how we can reclaim that lead.

As Reagan once said *without hesitation or doubt*: "It can be done."

Given the stakes, nationally and internationally, it simply must be done – but it won't be done if we stand idly by. This book sets forth the optimistic formula as to how Republicans can regain that lead – a formula validated by the history of American politics from Eisenhower to today.

As we embark on this journey, we must always remember that leadership never stands still. True leadership continues to forge ahead - rather than being content with past victories. Leadership is also a bit like driving a race car: If you do it looking over your shoulder too often, wondering if your competitor is closing ground - eventually you will crash. As we shall see in the pages ahead, the 2006 election was, in part, a lesson in the latter for Republicans.

In that light, it bears saying that this book was born of a bit of frustration. I began writing it in early 2005 after watching *Meet the Press*. Tim Russert interviewed the majority and minority leaders in the US Senate at the time, Democrat Senator Richard Durbin of Illinois and Republican Mitch McConnell of Kentucky. Durbin was advocating more spending. No surprise so far. Then Russert asked him something to the effect of "how are you going to pay" for that spending. Durbin read right off the Left's talking points and claimed that, because of the "Bush tax cuts," the US government could not afford Durbin's proposed spending programs. Still no surprise.

What did Senator McConnell say about the tax cuts in response? What did the then Minority Leader in the Senate – a man with vast experience since the tax-cutting days of the Reagan Revolution - say in rebuttal to Durbin's attack on the Bush tax cuts? Did he continue to forge ahead as Reagan would? Sadly, no. Indeed, McConnell said nothing about the tax cuts. Absolutely nothing. He let Durbin get away with it. It was as if he thought Durbin was right. Worse yet, it was if McConnell had forgotten how Reagan put Republicans ahead.

Of course, Durbin was, and the Democrats still are, wrong. At the time the Bush tax cuts were enacted, the nation was in a "Clinton-tax-increase-induced-9/11-exacerbated" recession – and, this just in Senator McConnell, recessions cause tax revenues to drop. On the flip side, since the Bush tax cuts were fully enacted in 2003, the US economy reversed its downward trend, roared back to life - and so have revenues: a 5% increase in '04, a 15% increase in 2005, a similar increase in 2006 and a large increase in 2007. Revenues have now *grown* by over $700 billion since the tax cuts – a record increase. Those increases are not unlike the revenue booms that occurred after the Reagan tax cuts, the Kennedy tax cuts, the Coolidge tax cuts and the many other examples in history when moribund economies were jumped-started with tax cuts.

As Republicans, Senator McConnell included, we need to be more than aware of that history. It needs to be a part of our vision, we need a strategy for its continued implementation and we must have the ability to articulate it when necessary. In large part, and in an effort to be **Silent No More**, that is why I wrote **The New Conservative Paradigm** and founded www.politicalvanguard.com – a conservative e-magazine.

Years ago, in the era when Democrats began "Blaming America First," Richard Nixon referred to many voters and volunteers who disagreed with that sentiment as the **Silent Majority** of American politics. He insisted that that the "silent majority" supported his efforts over those of the dissident Democrats.

Well for many of us today, we are s*ilent no more*. The frustrated and more fill the airways with talk radio calls, we write letters to the editor and otherwise volunteer in ever larger numbers.

We remember how Reagan broke our silence and how he boldly affirmed his beliefs and changed us, a nation and a world. We recognize that Reagan's greatest investment was in the American Spirit – our Spirit - not government - and we do not quite understand why the current crop of leaders will not live up to his calling. Others wonder if our current leaders truly understand the Reagan Revolution.

In rather simple terms, Reagan started a political realignment – a reversal of political fortunes – that lasted for more than two decades. Reagan did so not by wanting to *manage* government. Instead, Reagan was an inspirational *Leader* of *We the People* who changed the course of government.

Reagan did all of the above by championing what I call the 3 Pillars of *The New Conservative Paradigm:*

(1) Pro-Growth policies/reforms,

(2) Belief in America and her defense, and

(3) Respect for American Traditions and Values.

This book will chronicle not only that reversal of fortunes and the meaning of *The New Conservative Paradigm,* it also will feature its first messenger, Democrat John F. Kennedy, along with others that laid the groundwork for *The New Conservative Paradigm* and still others who strengthen *The New Conservative Paradigm.*

Finally, this book will also explore how the Republican Party can regain its lead in time for 2008 and how it can then stay ahead in what we shall see will be the difficult decade of 2010 to 2019. It is within that decade that the severe problems of our explosive growth in government will come home to roost – in the country as a whole and in many states, counties and cities as well.

If you are unconvinced that government growth is a problem, you need only to look at this chart to catch a glimpse of the unsustainable growth of our federal government.

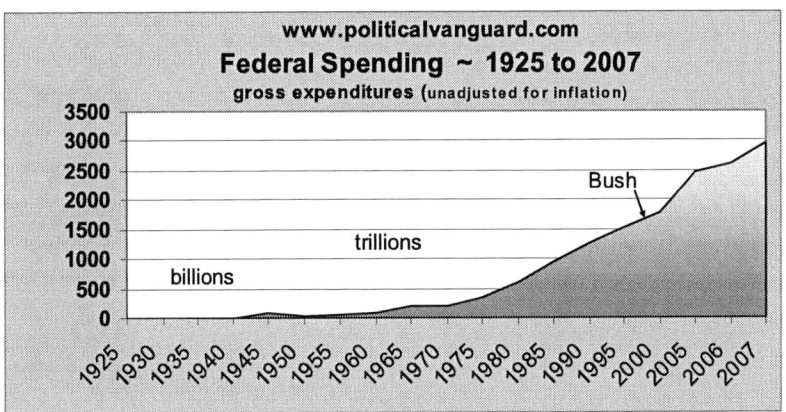

Federal spending, in gross terms (unadjusted for inflation), is 15 times the size it was just 35 years ago. It has more than doubled since 1995. We have no choice but to confront that growth. Fortunately, for those concerned, **Something Has Changed**.

SOMETHING HAS CHANGED

"Things do not change; *we change*."
Henry David Thoreau

Something has changed – indeed many things have changed. The Democrats of Zell Miller's[1] fond memories were the party of tax cuts. Those tax cuts are now the domain of the Republicans. From Franklin Roosevelt's "Arsenal of Democracy,"[2] the Democrats morphed into the party of disarmament and retreat – and with that transition - the Republicans became the Party most trusted with national defense.

Before that, and for almost 40 years, from the late 1950s to the mid 1990s, Congress was the playground of the Democrats who held perennial majorities. At their height, in 1965, the Democrats had the White House, a 295 – 140 majority in the House of Representatives and a 68 – 32 majority in the US Senate.

From 1994 to 2006, however, the Republican Party held sway in the halls of Congress. Further:

~ by 2008, Republicans will have held the White House in 28 of the last 39 years,

---

[1] During the 2004 Presidential campaign, Democrat Senator from Georgia Zell Miller became a National figure when he endorsed Republican George Bush for President over Democrat John Kerry. Miller also supported the Bush tax policies and gave a stirring speech at the 2004 Republican National Convention.

[2] In the midst of World War II, Franklin Roosevelt referred to Detroit's auto industry as the "Arsenal of Democracy" because it converted to war material production. The phrase was actually coined by a French businessman Jean Monnet – who used the phrase in a meeting with advisors of Roosevelt. Thereafter, he was asked not to use it again and it became the subject of one of Roosevelt's famous "fireside chats."

~ 97 of the 100 fastest growing counties in the country voted for President Bush in 2004,

~ In 2004, President George W. Bush became the first President in 16 years to get more than 50% of the vote,

~ President George W. Bush was the first President to increase his Party's representation in both Houses of Congress in three consecutive elections in over 50 years,

~ The Republican Party enjoyed over a decade of Congressional dominance in the House and Senate between 1994 and 2006,

~ In 2004, a majority of the US Governorships were held by Republicans, and

~ In 2004, the Republicans, for the first time in history, held the Governorships of the 4 largest states in the Country: California, New York, Florida and Texas.

Then, in 2006, some of those trends were reversed.

Did *things* change during those times? Or did *we* change? Regardless of whether you agree with Thoreau, and notwithstanding the 2006 elections, we are in a different age.

Where once an icon from our past told us "that's the way it is,"[3] unlikely media comets such as Dennis Miller, Christopher Hitchens, and Bill Cosby tell us the way it

---

[3] CBS' Walter Cronkite, once dubbed the most trusted man in America, signed off each night by reciting that phrase.

should be. Cable's Fox News lays claim to being fair and balanced, eclipses CNN regularly and even the networks on important stories such as political convention coverage.

For pure attitude and energy, Ann Coulter makes the cover of *Time* Magazine, while Michelle Malkin and Laura Ingraham, among others, hold the higher ground against the likes of whomever the Left puts up. Even in California, Conservative talk radio - featuring the bombastic in LA in the form of KFI's John and Ken to the more straightforward Dennis Prager, Hugh Hewitt and Larry Elder as well as Melanie Morgan and Lee Rodgers of KSFO in San Francisco - rule the airwaves while Air America, the liberals' attempt at a talk radio network, wallowed in bankruptcy before dropping off the air. Meanwhile, the Internet and its bloggers run roughshod over the *New York Times* and the *Boston Globe* – not to mention CBS.[4]

Even so, the question remains. Exactly what changed and how did it change? Did Republicans come up with better candidates for a period of time? More likable candidates? Better policies? The National Security Age/Homeland Security Age? Social issues? Economic Issues? Did they lose because of those things in 2006? Or is it all simply the turn of the wheel – each Party's turn in the sun?

---

[4] In the weeks before the 2004 election, CBS' and Dan Rather's hit piece regarding President Bush's military service was debunked by diligent bloggers.

Simply stated, there was a change – even if the 2005/2006 Congressional Republicans failed to notice the change - and any analysis of that change starts with President Ronald Reagan.

Years before the Reagan Presidency, during the early 1960s, the Democrats were in the lead and enjoyed huge majorities in Congress – majorities built in part on the tax cutting/pro-freedom ideas of John F. Kennedy. The Republicans, for their part, were the contrary party or the Party that said *No* - No to the Kennedy tax cuts (that's not a misprint) and *No* to the Great Society excesses of the Democrats as the decade wore on. It was a most unenviable position for the Republicans because the Democrats were buying votes with Great Society programs and earning votes with the Kennedy/Johnson tax cuts. The Republicans, on the other hand, did not have a positive message of their own, just a *contrary* message.

During the late 1960s and 1970s, the Democrats revived their New Deal role as the *Tax & Spend* Party and the Republicans became the "Tax and Spend-a-Little-Less Party." That still meant, however, that the Republicans were not really offering something – they were offering something *less*. All told, those "something less" messages earned the Republicans a solid *minority* position in Congress.

Enter Ronald Reagan – stage *right* or, as we shall come to find, from the theatre of the possible. From the ash heap of our national malaise under Jimmy Carter, arose candidate and then President Ronald Reagan.

Reagan was a champion of hope. At his core, Reagan believed in people not government. Amidst the struggles of the 1970s, Reagan well understood that our Nation would succeed not by falling back on more government intervention but by creating the conditions by which individuals, families and the American Spirit could move ahead.

Consistent with those beliefs, as President, Reagan sided with **We the People** over government. He enacted large, supply-side, personal income tax cuts and tax cuts for employers. Those tax cuts restored freedom to overburdened Americans – and in granting that freedom, Reagan energized a Nation. Not satisfied with that alone, Reagan sought to preserve freedom by championing government reform and he restricted the growth of government on whose leave freedom depends.

It was a *positive* agenda and his pro-growth/reform policies not only created an economic boom and cured America of its malaise, but they also restored America's sense of purpose and its pride. Simply stated, President Reagan became the national if not world purveyor of America's unique brand of **Optimism** – joining other great leaders of History who well understood that such a positive disposition is the father of political inspiration.

All of that was a winning formula because America, from the *Mayflower* to Microsoft, or if you like, from the *Santa Maria* to Schwarzenegger, has been about **Optimism**.

Reagan changed the dynamics of presidential politics as well. Since Reagan:

(1) All presidential candidates have been, and are now, defined by whether they are pro-growth or pro-government – or quite simply by their stance on taxes – the new fault-line of American politics;

(2) The *No New Tax Pledge* took hold;

(3) Presidential candidates either were for cutting taxes or suffered the consequences, and

(4) The Republicans became the majority Party in Congress – until they squandered that lead away in 2006.

That reformation of the national debate and of the national character was among the many changes History owes to Reagan. President George W. Bush, in no uncertain terms, at the outset of his Presidency embraced the policies and politics of optimism, tax cuts, freedom and the belief that we can achieve more.

For their part, the leadership of the Democrats appears not to be for anything – instead, they are *against* most everything: wars for freedom, tax cuts, social security reform,[5] and government reform in general, and, in California, Arnold Schwarzenegger's reforms for California in 2005.[6] So pure is their opposition mentality that despite the passage of months and months after the President and Schwarzenegger announced their 2005 reforms - the Democrats did not announce a single, meaningful counter-proposal. In the 2006 Congressional elections, the Democrats did not campaign with a platform and offered no positive agenda. Instead, they offered opposition to President Bush and the war in Iraq - and relied on the discontent of conservative and independent voters to win.

Once in power, in 2007, the Congressional Democrats accomplished little of note – a by-product of their empty, negative campaign that produced no mandate for a specific change – and, in doing so, House Leader Nancy Pelosi's Democrats presided over Congressional approval ratings of

---

[5] The President sought reform of the obviously troubled Social Security system in early 2005.

[6] In 2005, Governor Arnold Schwarzenegger proposed a series of reforms to the California legislature covering pension reform, paycheck-protection, education reform and redistricting reform. The Democrats legislature would not agree to make the reforms and that Fall, a special election was held on the reforms. Prior to that, at no time did the Democrats in the legislature seriously offer reforms of their own. The reforms did not pass due to a combination of voter fatigue in California (it was the 4th election in 4 years), a marginal bias against initiatives, Republicans' failure to vote in Southern California strongholds, a massive - if not unprecedented - union campaign against the Governor personally, conservative disenchantment over spending in Washington and the combination of measures which resulted in a united liberal opposition to them all.

historic lows. As such, it is fair to say that the Democrats are the Party of criticism not suggestion – or, the Party of No.

In the final analysis, the Democrat leadership, nationally and in state after state, does not embrace **Optimism** nor reform, nor lower taxes. To the contrary, the philosophy of the Democrat leadership can be distilled into this simple paradigm:

> **If you make it - they will take it**
> **- and if you don't have it -**
> **they have a program for it.**

In other words, their philosophy is to punish those who succeed and to promote dependency. They believe not in self-reliance, but in government programs. Indeed, it would appear that they prefer that the government safety net become a hammock – all of which amounts to nothing more than a throwback to the days of buying votes with government handouts. It is a negative agenda filled with yesterday's ideas and an agenda that was badly losing in the battle for the hearts and minds of American voters – until the Republican Leaders forgot the lessons of the Reagan Revolution and lost their way in the years before the 2006 election.

In the coming pages, we will focus on the changes fostered by the Reagan Revolution. Those changes, however, are not the end of our analysis, but instead, the beginning. It is so, because pro-growth policies, although the dominant governing policy, were not the only governing themes of Ronald Reagan. President Reagan also managed a reversal of fortunes between the two parties on the issue of who is fighting for our families and their traditions. He also solidified the Republicans' lead as protectors of the American homeland. In doing all of that, and by transforming the national debate and the national character, Reagan established a *New Conservative Paradigm* and inspired *New Conservatives*.

In order to truly appreciate the Reagan Revolution, however, it will be important to truly understand more than just the changes Reagan set in motion. We must understand his part - in light of the whole – and we especially must understand what came before Reagan: the Soul of a "Me Too" Party – so that Republicans never become so again.

THE SOUL OF A "ME TOO" PARTY

"Mondale has the soul of a vice president."
Sen. Eugene McCarthy 1976

Long before "powerful" Vice Presidents such as Dick Cheney, or Al Gore, Vice-Presidents were to be seen, not heard. They had a soul – too often vacant. Minority parties, at times, have had that vacant soul as well. It is important to note that they don't just wake up one day as the minority party – they get to be that the old-fashioned way – *they earn it*. And so it was for the Republican Party, lackluster for more than two decades - from the late fifties through the sixties and into the late seventies.

The Numbers Don't Lie

In 1953, Republican Gen. Dwight D. Eisenhower was President. The Republicans controlled the House of Representatives and the US Senate. In the House, Republicans outnumbered Democrats 221 to 213 with one Independent. The Republicans held a slim majority in the Senate, 48 – 46 with 2 independents.

It would be 42 years before Republicans would again lay claim to that majority status in the House.

In between:

~ No less than three times, or for six years, the Democrats would have more than *twice* as many House Members as the Republicans (1965: 295 - 140), (1975: 291 – 144), (1977: 292 – 143).

~ Six times, or for a total of twelve years, the Democrats had at least *100* more members in the House than the Republicans: (1959, 1965, 1975, 1979, 1983, 1991).[7]

The Republicans fared not much better in the US Senate. After the 1954 election, the Democrats held a slim one (1) seat advantage, 48 – 47, (with one Independent) in the Senate. In the aftermath of the 1957/58 Eisenhower recession, that advantage became wide and deep – jumping to a 64 to 34 advantage after the 1958 election. Six (6) times thereafter, the Democrats sat more than 60 US Senators in the US Congress - reaching a high of 68 Senate Seats after the 1964 election.

It's rather hard to argue with those numbers or their message: The Republicans were the minority party in Congress for years upon years after "controlling" the White House, the House of Representatives and the Senate in 1953.

The only question is why. Fortunately, the answer is plain enough, at least to the new conservatives.

The Road to Minority*hood*
"Affordable Tax Cuts" – The Eisenhower Years

To say that the Republicans controlled the White House in 1953 is factually correct but perhaps overstated in effect.

---

[7] Compare that to 2005's "slim" 30 seat Republican House majority which many viewed as a significant margin.

Republican Dwight Eisenhower was not a staunch Republican by any modern standards.

Indeed, four years before he accepted the Republican nomination, two Democrats, Claude Pepper and James Roosevelt, attempted to woo Eisenhower to run for the 1948 *Democratic* nomination. Eisenhower, however, did not accept their overtures. Instead, Eisenhower decided to seek, and ultimately win the Republican nomination in 1952.

Obviously, history hardly indicates that Eisenhower was philosophically well-defined. Could you imagine the Democrats asking Reagan to be their nominee in 1980? No, Eisenhower was a popular war hero. He was the former Supreme Allied Commander in Europe and Commander of NATO – not a doctrinaire politician committed to an agenda. That was all too clear when it came to taxes.

Despite a landslide victory for Republicans in 1952, in what would become a familiar signpost along the **Road to Minorityhood** for Republicans, Eisenhower remained politically and economically cautious. On the issue of taxes, Eisenhower early on would declare:

"We cannot *afford* to reduce taxes, reduce income until we have in sight a program of expenditure that shows that the factors of income and outgo will be balanced."

In Eisenhower's 1954 State-of-the-Union, he again made his aversion to tax cuts very clear. Eisenhower stated:

"Six days ago individual income taxes were reduced and the excess profits tax expired.

"These tax reductions are justified <u>only</u> because of the substantial reductions we already have made and are making in governmental expenditures. As additional reductions in expenditures are brought gradually but surely into sight, further reductions in taxes can and will be made.

"When budget savings and sound governmental financing are assured, tax burdens should be reduced so that taxpayers may spend their own money in their own way."

His commitment to tax cuts was muddled but his message quite clear. Tax cuts are *only* justifiable if the **government can afford** to cut them, i.e. if the government hasn't otherwise spent the money – only then may taxpayers keep and spend their own money. It was a two-part equation and ***government spending was paramount over private tax relief***. It was a policy that sided with the needs of government over the inspirational freedom of **We the People**.

Beyond that, tax relief seemingly was not an instrument of economic policy - let alone a powerful means for generating growth. Instead, it was to be tolerated politically if spending was controlled.

Perhaps what is most remarkable to readers of today, about Eisenhower's statement in his 1954 State of the Union address is: (1) that it was made in the midst of a recession and (2) the top personal income tax rate was 91% at the time. Faced with such a suffocating tax rate, between July 1953 and May 1954, there was a 2.7% ***decline*** in real US GDP.

Eisenhower was obviously unmoved by the recession and instead was primarily focused on balancing the federal budget during the economic downturn.

Eisenhower's reluctance to cut taxes during a recession, however economically wrong, was not unheard of at the time. To the contrary, Republican President Hoover, in 1930, well after the stock market crash of October 1929, and amidst a recession, raised the top personal tax rate from 25% to 63%. That tax increase helped foster the Great Depression, caused federal revenues to decline and set Republicans back politically for years to come. Why would Hoover take such action? Why would Hoover choose the concerns of government over the needs of the American people during a bad recession? Because he too mistakenly believed that raising tax rates, as opposed to fostering economic growth, was the path to balancing the federal budget. For his part, Democrat FDR continued that misguided policy and later raised the top rate to 79% - an act that prolonged the Great Depression.

Returning our attention to Eisenhower, what was less remarkable, or perhaps more predictable, was that Eisenhower faced a second, more severe, recession just three years later in 1958. That fall, the Democrats gained 15 seats in the US Senate. That election made it clear that the war hero was not an economic hero. Less than two years later, a third recession hit and the US was ready for a change away from a cautious manager of government in favor of a vibrant Leader.

The Road To Minorityhood Continues With . . . A Contrast in All Respects

President Eisenhower was, by all measures, cautious. His leadership style has been variously described as "oblique"[8] and "easy going." "He took his party to the center of the road, 'where the traction is best and where you can bring the most people along with you.' His critics saw his "middle way" as one without the vision or courage to engage the important social issues of the day."[9] The election of JFK, in the fall of 1960, would change all that.

Whether or not you were a fan of the new President, the contrast between Eisenhower the manager and John F. Kennedy the leader could not be more pronounced – not only in style – but demonstrably when it came to taxes and economic growth – and *Optimism*.

Kennedy confronted the stagnant economic times of the late 1950s by asking Americans, in his campaign, to confront

---

[8] Fred Greenstein DWIGHT EISENHOWER AND THE HIDDEN-HAND PRESIDENCY

[9] Dwight Eisenhower, The Cautious Warrior, http://www.historywise.com/KoTrain/Courses/DE/DE_Domestic_Affairs.htm

the "New Frontier." He faced a tax system that, in 1962, required the top one percent to pay a whopping 20 percent of all income taxes. The top marginal rate was still that incredible 91% - meaning that for every additional dollar that taxpayer made, 91¢ of it went to the federal government.

Boldly, President Kennedy set a course 180° away from his predecessor on the issue of taxes. From the article "Sorry Ted: JFK cut taxes" by W. James Antle III, we read:

"Kennedy call[ed] for 'an across-the-board, top-to-bottom cut in personal and corporate income taxes.' He argued 'that our present tax system ... exerts too heavy a drag on growth ... siphons out of the private economy too large a share of personal and business purchasing power, [and] reduces the financial incentives for personal effort, investment, and risk-taking.

Kennedy explicitly endorsed rate reductions for high-income taxpayers in language that foreshadowed supply-side economics, proposing tax cuts '**for those in the middle and upper brackets, who can thereby be encouraged to undertake additional efforts and ... invest more capital.**"[10]

In his January 24, 1963 message to Congress, Kennedy completed the revolution in thought by stating:

"I repeat: our practical choice is not between a tax-cut deficit and budgetary surplus. It is between two kinds of deficits: a chronic deficit of inertia, as the unwanted result of inadequate revenues and a restricted economy; or a temporary deficit of transition, resulting from a **tax cut**

---

[10] http://www.enterstageright.com/archive/articles/0301jfk.htm

designed to boost the economy, increase tax revenues, and achieve--and I believe this can be done--a budget surplus."

Just weeks before that, Kennedy declared his pro-growth, supply side *Optimistic* beliefs in earnest by stating:

"It is a paradoxical truth that tax rates are too high today and tax revenues are too low and the soundest way to raise the revenues *in the long run* is to cut tax rates now."[11]

As you read those words, it is more than apparent that Kennedy would be no Eisenhower. Gone was any notion that tax cuts were a political luxury to be *afforded* only if government spending was under control. Gone was any discussion of spending at all. The issue was no longer a two-part equation. Replacing such intellectual inertia was the prospect of "a temporary deficit of transition," the result of a tax cut designed to "*increase* tax revenues." **Taxes became a one-part equation – an economic policy instrument for growth**.

In his gallant style and with sheer *Optimism*, Kennedy sided with *We the People* over government and declared that tax cuts *not tax increases* were the way to balance the budget – the complete opposite of Republican Hoover, Democrat Roosevelt, Democrat Truman and Republican Eisenhower. How would tax cuts do that? They would do

---

[11] Kennedy speech to the Economic Club of New York, December 14, 1962.

so by restoring freedom to Americans and by fostering economic growth. It was Regan*esque* before Reagan. Indeed, it was Kennedy*esque* – and along with his strong defense of America and its ideals - warrants recognizing JFK as **The First New Conservative**. It was also more than just an economic policy. The transition from Eisenhower to Kennedy was a dynamic change in philosophy and momentum.

Indeed, the tax cuts were but one small aspect of the ***Optimistic***, can-do aspect of Kennedy's brief tenure. On the issue of world peace, Kennedy proclaimed he was seeking a broader achievement:

"What kind of peace do I mean? What kind of peace do we seek? Not a Pax Americana enforced on the world by American weapons of war. Not the peace of the grave or the security of the slave.

"I am talking about genuine peace, the kind of peace that makes life on earth worth living, the kind that enables men and nations to grow and to hope and to build a better life for their children -- not merely peace for Americans but peace for all men and women -- not merely peace in our time, but peace in all time."

Kennedy renewed the call for the US to land a man on the moon – not someday but *before the decade was out*. He founded the Peace Corps and boldly claimed in the face of the Soviet Union: "All free men, wherever they may live, are citizens of Berlin, and, therefore, as a free man, I take pride in the words 'Ich bin ein Berliner.'"

In those and other respects, *Kennedy's Camelot* was not synonymous with *Eisenhower's Caution*. The leader of the Democrats was young, ambitious and **Optimistic** – and he had an economic policy to match it – tax cuts that could "achieve" growth.

History, or more accurately, his assassination, did not allow Kennedy to see his agenda enacted and, in the long run, that would result in the Democrats becoming a minority party. In the short run, and in an odd historical twist, his **Optimistic** agenda was adopted by a Vice-President turned President who hardly represented Camelot.

President Lyndon Johnson was no John Kennedy. He was older, much less charismatic, and embodied little of Kennedy's gallant style. Nevertheless, Johnson sought the enactment of Kennedy's agenda: At the outset of his 1964 State-of-the-Union, Johnson declared:

"Let us carry forward the plans and programs of John Fitzgerald Kennedy -- not because of our sorrow or sympathy, but because **they are right**.

On the issue of tax cuts, Johnson posited that:

[E]very individual American taxpayer and every corporate taxpayer will benefit from the earliest possible passage of the pending tax bill from both the new investment it will bring and the new jobs that it will create."

By making that statement, Johnson appeared to accept and understand the pro-growth nature of the proposed tax cut – but did he really think that Kennedy's programs were right? The answer, as the unfolding years would demonstrate, was no. Indeed, by his very next statement, any understanding or commitment to pro-growth tax policies was belied – a statement which demonstrated that the Democrats had lost their *Optimistic* Leader and replaced him with someone more managerial and economically cautious, someone more like Eisenhower. Indeed the seeds of a future Reversal of Party Fortunes were sown when Johnson went on to say:

"That tax bill has been thoroughly discussed for a year. Now we need action. **The new budget clearly allows it.**"

Such a statement was reflective of a long-time tax and spend legislator and *Eisenhower could not have said it much better – tax cuts were acceptable because the government could afford them*. Once again, *We the People* were subordinated to the needs of government.

To Be Contrary or Right?

At the time of Johnson's State-of-the-Union request for a tax cut in 1964, the Republicans had a clear choice: whether to be *right* or whether to be *contrary*. Given Johnson's ambiguous message on tax cuts, it would have been possible to grab the ***Optimistic*** mantle of pro-growth leadership away from Johnson and the Democrats and to come down on the side of individuals and families. The Republican leadership, however, chose to be largely *contrary*.

In fact, Republicans in significant numbers opposed the Kennedy/Johnson tax cuts – including Barry Goldwater who called the cuts "gimmickry" during the 1964 Presidential campaign. Later in the campaign, in a reversal, Goldwater proposed his own set of tax cuts. His characterization of the Kennedy cuts as "gimmickry," however, made it impossible for Republicans to get out in front of the issue and many wound up opposing the Kennedy/Johnson cuts. Obviously, that left the voters without a clear message of whether the Republicans understood the purpose or value of tax cuts.[12]

Time proved that to be contrary and/or ambivalent was to be wrong and Kennedy to be right.

Over the next three years, the Kennedy/Johnson tax cuts produced annual growth rates in excess of 5% from 1964 to 1967. Combined with Johnson's Great Society, the Democrats got the credit for the tax cuts and appeared to have cornered the national political market: Tax cuts for

---

[12] To some degree, perhaps, the Republicans of the early 1960s can be forgiven in their opposition to tax cuts. American economic history was not as clear as it was by 1967. As we shall see, the Republicans would have no such excuse by 1967 and certainly none today.

those paying taxes, including individuals and business owners, and social programs for the middle and lower economic classes.

Committed to Minorityhood, The Republican Party of "Me Too" Emerges

In 1965, the Kennedy/Johnson Democrats enjoyed huge majorities in Congress: a 295 to 140 margin in the House and a 68 to 32 majority in the Senate. Faced with the popular (and effective) tax cuts, as well as popular spending programs, for their part, the Republicans developed a message deficit – they were at first the party of "No." Many opposed the Kennedy/Johnson tax cuts on the grounds of fiscal responsibility. Most opposed the spending increases of the Great Society on the same grounds. But that left them with very little to offer voters, no positive message of their own – just a *contrary* message.

How did the Republicans handle that message deficit as the decade wore on? What would they do in the wake of Johnson's decision not to run a second time and Nixon's victory? They simply failed to seize the opening. In some respects, the Republican Party chose to dig an even deeper hole even though large political opportunities presented themselves.

The first such opportunity came in 1967. Consistent with his Eisenhower-like wariness of tax cuts, and notwithstanding the success of the Kennedy tax cut programs, starting in 1967, President Johnson pursued a tax *increase* which was signed into law in 1968. It purportedly was needed "pay" for the Vietnam War and the Democrats' Great Society spending. In other words, and rather incredibly, despite increasing federal revenues generated by an economy growing by five percent or more a year, President Johnson and the Democrats unilaterally disarmed themselves on the issue of tax cuts. They had resumed their New Deal tax and spend ways and newly titled them as the War on Poverty and the Great Society.[13] Moreover, it was also clear that the Democrats no longer had an ***Optimistic*** pro-growth leader of ***We the People*** but instead a proponent of the needs of government.

At that moment, in the race for political leadership, the Republicans clearly were behind the Democrats in Congress and among voters as far as party affiliation. Logically, therefore, in order to overtake the Democrats, the Republicans running for Congress would need to offer voters something other than what the Democrats were offering –

---

[13] In his 1964 State of the Union speech, Johnson dubbed his request for social welfare spending a War on Poverty. Those programs were part of Johnson's Great Society – a series of federal programs promoted by the Democrats to eliminate poverty and racial injustice.

otherwise voters would not have a compelling reason to vote the Congressional Democrats out. The Republicans needed to offer better policies at the same time they exposed the weakness of the Democrats policies. In that way, defeating an incumbent party is no different than defeating a single incumbent politician.

It is within that context that the clear tax cut opening had emerged for the Republicans. The Republicans, however, failed to seize that opening.

It did not have to be so. By then, the lessons of the Kennedy cuts were plain to see: The economy was performing brilliantly and tax revenues were on the rise. That experience could be matched with the lessons of the tax cuts of the early 1920s. Back then, **Republican** Calvin Coolidge cut the top personal income rate from 71% to 24%. The economy responded and grew 59% - a phenomenon dubbed *The Roaring 20s*.

Armed with that knowledge, the Republicans of the mid 1960s still did not become the Party of tax cuts. To the contrary, they would become the "Me Too" party.

Indeed, history recorded that in 1967, the Republicans did not make a name for themselves through opposition to the Johnson tax increase. In 1969, despite winning the White House with President Nixon, the Republicans would do no better. Nixon responded to what was becoming a growing economic inflationary crisis by adopting the position of the *Democrats* at the time. Nixon and the Democrat led Congress sided with government over *We the People* and *increased* taxes by doubling the capital gains rate – as anti-growth a tax measure as you can dream up – all in a renewed effort to reduce the deficit – **not by cutting taxes but by raising tax rates.**

Nixon also cemented his role as a champion of government solutions by pulling nearly every lever of government he could to address the growing economic problem - rather than freeing up Americans to do the job. Nixon's efforts included imposing wage and price controls. But even that was not all, on the spending side, under Nixon and the Democrat Congress, "entitlement spending grew from 6.5 percent of GDP in 1969 to 10.6 percent in 1975, an unprecedented increase."[14]

With that combination, Congressional Republicans, led by President Nixon, chose the worst of all political worlds – behind the Democrats in the race for Congress and offering the voters virtually the same domestic policies - they truly had become the "Me Too" party. They too were the party of tax increases, government and higher spending – and to no real political avail. Two years after Nixon's 1968 victory, in the 1970 Congressional election, the Democrats still won

---

[14] Do These Deficits Look Familiar? *Jonathan Rauch* http://www.reason.com/rauch/012604.shtml

255 House seats, the Republicans 180 – all because they offered the voters no meaningful alternative to the Democrats.

In 1972, Nixon won in a landslide: 61% to 38% in the popular vote and 520 – 17 in the Electoral College. Despite that historically successful Presidential election, however, the gap between Democrats and the Democrat–lite-Republicans closed to only 242 Democrats and 192 Republicans in Congress - and that narrowing proved short-lived. In the aftermath of Watergate,[15] the margin ballooned again, in 1974, to 291 Democrats and 144 Republicans.

Thus, by the early 1970s, and despite two Presidential victories, the Republicans emerged as largely the same as the Democrats – a "Me Too Party" on spending and a Party that supported anti-growth tax policies. Such lesser policies and lack of leadership would not and did not change the political dynamic of the time - the Republicans would remain the distinctly minority Party.

The Ford Presidency provided little more inspiration to voters.

Ford inherited the tax-increasing, high spending policies of Johnson and Nixon. Those policies left the country with a growing economic crisis. The catch phrase for that crisis was something called "stagflation." It referred to the prevailing economic condition of the time: low economic

---

[15] Nixon resigned on August 8, 1974.

growth rates, rising consumer prices and a weak labor market. Normally, lower growth rates tend to lead to a softening of prices. However, during this period of time, inflation surged – due in large part to poor governmental monetary policy that caused increases in the Consumer Price Index.

What did President Ford do in response? Ford sought spending cuts and a $50 rebate for taxpayers – yet another non-pro-growth tax bill given that it provided no future economic incentives. Instead, it was a "reward" and a paltry one at that, for a prior years' activity. The economy, for its part, did not respond as Ford hoped. Inflation remained historically high and economic growth continued to be anemic.

In the November Presidential election of 1976, President Ford lost to a peanut farmer from Georgia, Jimmy Carter. It is, of course, conventional wisdom that Ford lost that election because of his pardon of Richard Nixon in the wake of Watergate. Surely, Watergate and the ensuing pardon hobbled Ford and the Republicans heading into the 1976 election. Despite that, Ford nearly caught Carter at the end.

Given that, was Watergate and the pardon really the reason Ford lost or was it something else? In truth it was something else: the very bad economic condition that the tax increasing, big spending Nixon laid at Ford's feet. It was a storyline that Ford did little to turn around. As they went to the polls, voters well noticed that poor economic condition of the country over the previous two years which included unemployment as high as 9% and inflation that topped 12%. The question remains, therefore, what would have become of Gerald Ford if he had given voters an alternate, compelling economic storyline?

Ford didn't give them that other storyline and the Republican Party, in the meantime, still had no strong separate identity from the Democrats - unless you consider spending a little less than the Democrats wanted (Ford vetoed an average of 26.4 bills per year) and taxing along with the Democrats as passing for a political identity. In that same November of 1976, the Democrats claimed 292 House seats – their second highest total since the Roosevelt years – and 61 Senate seats.

Taking Stock ~ Part I

As we take stock of the two decades we have just reviewed, it is hard to ignore the pattern that emerges. Again, the cautious manager Eisenhower, perhaps the father of *affordable* tax cuts, laid claim to a Republican majority in the House and Senate at the beginning of his Presidency. However, as he presided over marginal tax rates of 91%, erroneously designed to satisfy the needs of government at the expense of initiative, Eisenhower endured three recessions and Republicans eventually gave way to the pro-growth/pro-citizen Kennedy Democrats. By 1964, factors which included the Kennedy/Johnson marginal rate tax cuts program helped build a 295 to 140 Democrat majority in the House. Once enacted, the tax cuts would soon have the economy booming.

By 1968, however, the Democrats' disarray under Johnson, which included a muted voice for pro-growth policies along with anti-war protests, led to the election of Nixon and a temporary narrowing of the divide. But the anti-growth/tax and spend policies of the Republicans from 1969 to 1975, along with Watergate, once again cemented the Republicans' minority status, 291 seats to 144 seats, as the chart below displays.

As anyone can plainly see, the largest Republican losses occurred during Eisenhower's and Nixon's anti-growth administrations and when Republicans opposed or were ambivalent about pro-growth policies, i.e. the Kennedy's tax cuts.

Party Divisions in the House of Representatives from 1953 to 1977

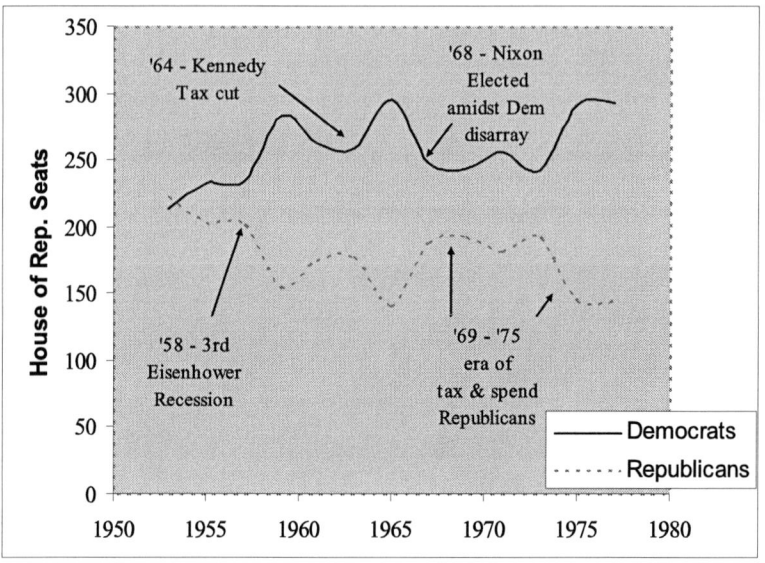

The Senate elections followed a similar pattern during the same period. The Democrats reached a high of 64 seats during the second Eisenhower recession and then bettered that by winning 67 seats in the 1962 election and 68 seats in the 1964 election, i.e. during the time of the Kennedy pro-growth policies. Republicans would close the gap amidst the Democrats disarray in the late 1960s but would squander their gains with tax and spend policies. Those failed policies and Watergate would lead to the Democrats claiming 61 Senate seats in the 1974 election.

US Senate Breakdown from 1953 to 1977

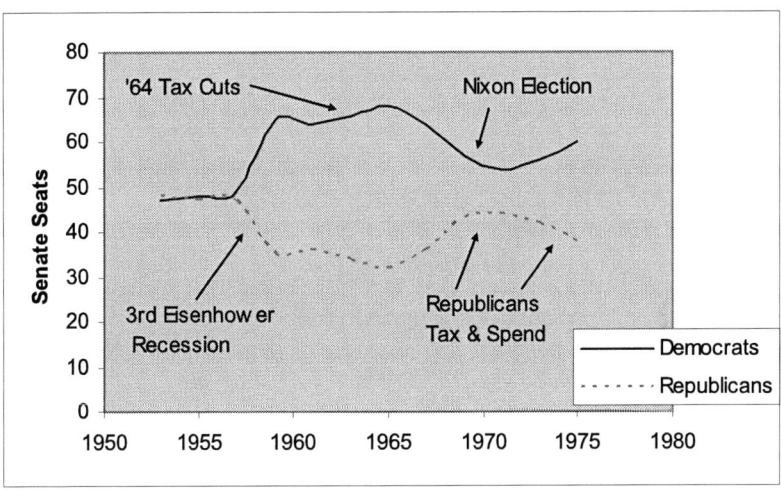

Such political fortunes would change, however, with a grand curve on a cocktail napkin and a Great Communicator.

HOPE MATTERS

"A Leader is a Dealer in Hope."
Napoleon

"We are too great a nation to limit ourselves to small dreams."
Ronald Reagan

Historians have sometimes quarreled as to whether the man creates the times or the times create the man. As the close of the seventies drew near, if nothing else, it was apparent that Ronald Reagan was the right man at the right time.

The late sixties and seventies brought the United States unprecedented challenges, social upheaval, unwanted new vocabulary and perhaps worst of all, a sense of diminished expectations. The Vietnam War separated the Country like no other war since the Civil War. The Pentagon Papers and the Watergate Cover-up challenged people's faith in their government. "Stagflation" entered the public lexicon in earnest along with something called the "Misery Index"[16] and an "Islamic Fundamentalist" revolution that held Americans hostage.[17]

For the prior sixteen years, the Nation endured an extended period of less than inspiring Presidents – all of whom managed government to achieve social ends: Lyndon Johnson, who declined to run for a second term, Richard Nixon who resigned, President Ford – a President never elected, and then Jimmy Carter, who endured a hostage crisis

---

[16] Republicans referred to the combination of the unemployment and inflation indexes under President Jimmy Carter as the "Misery Index." Under Carter, unemployment topped 7% and inflation rose above 13%. The prime interest rate reached a high of 21.5%.

[17] Under President Jimmy Carter, the US embassy in Iran was overtaken by radical Iranian "students" which held Americans hostage for 444 days only to be freed as Reagan became President.

helplessly and then watched, if not directed our nation into a period of national malaise.

The 1980 election would change all that. In much the same manner that JFK's election reinvigorated the nation after three recessions under Eisenhower, Ronald Reagan's election offered a wearied nation a fresh start from Carter's malaise.

The Language of Despair Replaced by Hope.

The near-complete unraveling of the Carter Presidency occurred on the night of July 15, 1979. It was on that night that he gave his infamous "malaise" speech. Carter appeared to question Americans' resolve in a manner that seemed more appropriate to questioning his own. The seminal moment in his speech came when he said:

"I want to talk to you right now about a fundamental threat to American democracy. I do not mean our political and civil liberties. They will endure. And I do not refer to the outward strength of America, a nation that is at peace tonight everywhere in the world, with unmatched economic power and military might.

"The threat is nearly invisible in ordinary ways. It is a crisis of confidence. It is a crisis that strikes at the very heart and soul and spirit of our national will. We can see this crisis in the growing doubt about the meaning of our own lives and in the loss of a unity of purpose for our Nation.

The erosion of our confidence in the future is threatening to destroy the social and the political fabric of America."

By an electoral margin of 489 to 49, in November of 1980, the American people, however, decided that the erosion in confidence was in Jimmy Carter and replaced him with Ronald Reagan. Once again, American history was witness to a dramatic change in style, substance and spirit.

Despite precious little change in the economy or world affairs from the time of Carter's malaise speech, Reagan served notice in his 1980 address to his nomination convention that success was possible. In reading these words, we must remember that leading up to the Reagan Presidency, the succession of Johnson, Nixon, Ford and Carter produced such a loss in confidence in Presidents that some skeptics doubted that the US or its Presidency could be managed by just one person.

Unbowed by such skeptics, a confident Reagan turned about face from Carter's disappointments and, quoting Thomas Paine, declared: "We have it in our power to begin the world over again."

Reagan continued by stating:

"Nearly 150 years after Tom Paine wrote those words, an American president told the generation of the Great Depression that it had a "rendezvous with destiny." I believe that this generation of Americans today has a rendezvous with destiny . . . The time is now, my fellow Americans, to recapture our destiny, to take it into our own hands."

Several months later, in his Inauguration speech, Reagan continued his uplifting theme and summoned a nation to greatness once again:

"It is time for us to realize that we are too great a nation to limit ourselves to small dreams. We're not, as some would have us believe, doomed to an inevitable decline. I do not believe in a fate that will fall on us no matter what we do. I do believe in a fate that will fall on us if we do nothing.

So with all the creative energy at our command, let us begin an era of national renewal. Let us renew our determination, our courage, and our strength. And let us renew our faith and our hope. We have every right to dream heroic dreams."

The difference between Carter's malaise and Reagan's hope was not just a change in speech writers. It was not just a change between a fallen President and a Leader. It was a manifestation of Reagan's fundamental understanding that great Leaders are Dealers in Hope, they are **Optimists** and they *engage their constituents in a higher purpose.* Such is the history of the great American Presidents George Washington and Abraham Lincoln.

Washington and Lincoln:
Leadership by Higher Purpose

Before the end of the Revolutionary War, there were those who wanted George Washington to become King of what would become these United States.[18] But Washington, who was revered for his character, had a higher purpose – not just for himself, but for his country. "Washington had the vision of an independent, republican, constitutional government controlled by a free people. He also envisioned this nation as contributing to the uplifting and happiness in the years, even centuries, to come of the whole world."[19]

Indeed, Washington had great expectations for his Country:

"As Mankind becomes more liberal, they will be more apt to allow that all those who conduct themselves as worthy members of the community are equally entitled to the protections of civil government. *I hope ever to see America among the foremost nations of justice and liberality.*"[20]

---

[18] RICHARD BROOKHISER ON GEORGE WASHINGTON, http://www.pbs.org/newshour/gergen/brookhiser.html

[19] **Richard C. Stazesky**, GEORGE WASHINGTON, GENIUS IN LEADERSHIP, http://gwpapers.virginia.edu/articles/stazesky.html

[20] Note Washington's use of the word "liberality." He uses it in its original sense – the state of being free – not in the sense liberal Democrats would use it in the 1900s.

Combined with his moral standing, it is little wonder that he became the Commander in Chief of the Continental Army, President of the Constitutional Convention and first President of the Country"

In accepting the latter, and relinquishing it after two terms, just as he relinquished his military power at the end of the Revolutionary War, Washington stood in the breach of history. He could have sought his own realm and thwarted the world's experiment with democracy – but instead, he remained principled, made the untested Constitution real, and with his brand of ***Optimism*** inspired the rest of History. It is for that leadership that Washington must be counted among History's absolute greatest.

That legacy of the first George W. is the same ideal that the current George W. wanted to foster when he dubbed the current century, "the century of liberty."[21] Long before Bush's freedom wars, however, Lincoln called upon a Country to save that ideal.

Lincoln Dies for the Last Best Hope

Contemporary Americans simply cannot know the magnitude of the difficulties that faced President Lincoln and, indeed, the young Nation. "By the time Lincoln arrived

---

[21] "I believe we're living in a century that will be called the century of liberty." President George W. Bush, on the 2004 campaign trial.

in Washington to be sworn in as the Nation's 16th president, 4 Mar. 1861, the Confederate States of America had been formed."[22] Lincoln rose to the office of the Presidency after just a single term in the House of Representatives and a failed Senate run against Stephen A. Douglas.

In that short time, however, Lincoln had made more than a name for himself because of his opposition to the most divisive issue in American history: slavery – an issue that not only divided the Northern and Southern states – but also the Democrat Party into a Northern Faction and a Southern Faction.[23] Riding that division and his growing stature, Lincoln was elected President and some Southern states responded by seceding from the Union.

Thus, Lincoln was faced not with one crisis but two crises that were intertwined: (1) a fractured country and (2) the growing chorus in favor of ending the horror of slavery - either of which would dwarf the problems of 2006 America.

Within weeks of his inauguration, the Civil War began at Fort Sumter, Charleston Harbor, South Carolina. For over a year, the disparate sides fought America's most costly battles. In December of 1862, in his annual message to Congress, Lincoln called on his nation not just to save the already fractured Union, but to an even higher purpose:

---

[22] Historical Times Encyclopedia of the Civil War, http://www.civilwarhome.com/lincolnbio.htm.

[23] Just over 100 years later, a war would divide the Democrats again and lead to a Republican Presidential victory. That war? The Vietnam war.

"Fellow-citizens, we cannot escape history. We of this Congress and this administration will be remembered in spite of ourselves. No personal significance, or insignificance, can spare one or another of us. The fiery trial through which we pass, will light us down, in honor or dishonor, to the latest generation.

We say we are for the Union. The world will not forget that we say this. We know how to save the Union. The world knows we do know how to save it. We—even we here—hold the power, and bear the responsibility.

In giving freedom to the slave, we assure freedom to the free—honorable alike in what we give, and what we preserve. We shall nobly save, or meanly lose, the last best, hope of earth."

It would be several years before the South's bid for independence and slavery were vanquished. In the end, Lincoln lost his life in the fight to give freedom to others. By persevering though the vicissitudes of a Civil War, he saved a nation. By prevailing against slavery, he ensured not only his place in History as one of America's greatest Presidents, but America's place in History as a place of justice and liberality - indeed the last best *hope* of earth.

It was not mere coincidence that Washington and Lincoln, in difficult times, called upon Americans to fight not just for the war at hand. Instead, Washington and Lincoln challenged Americans to look beyond themselves, to achieve something greater than victory. They inspired a young nation to fight for and achieve justice, liberality, freedom and, of course, hope – not for them alone but for mankind as a whole. Those ideals, even though achieved with blood-soaked memories, were *positive* goals designed to lift up the Nation. Call it leadership by **Higher Purpose**.

Although many other Presidents have made reference to those ideals, Washington and Lincoln walk nearly alone because they shepherded a war-torn Nation through its most difficult hours – not by turning the concerns of the Nation inward, but instead, by challenging it to achieve a greater good.

Over a Century later, faced with crises of a different proportion, that lesson would not be lost on Ronald Reagan.

REAGAN ACHIEVES OUR HEROIC DREAMS

"We will be as a city upon a hill."
Ronald Reagan *quoting* John Winthrop

When the Reagan Presidency began, the nation was faced with economic troubles, a crisis in confidence and a decades-old Cold War. When Reagan announced his candidacy for President, he placed blame for those problems not in the impossibilities of the time, but on the failings of its leaders:

"The crisis we face is not the result of any failure of the American spirit; it is the failure of our leaders to establish rational *goals* and give our people something to order their lives by."

In his first inaugural address, Reagan asked the Nation to "renew our faith and our *hope*." Reagan was certain that, as a Nation, *"We have every right to dream heroic dreams."* He also made it quite clear that "there [would] be no misunderstanding -- we're going to begin to act beginning today."

Rational goals would take the form of two broad initiatives designed as much to restore America's confidence as they were the political/economic problems of the day. Reagan proposed to invigorate the economy. He also proposed a military build-up. In time, it could fairly be said that both were designed to restore America, her standing in the world and to hasten the demise of the Soviet Union.

Reagan Takes On Economic Stagnation

If the economy was not working, it cannot be a surprise that Reagan wanted to empower individual Americans to make it work. Thus, after thwarting an assassin's bullet on March 30, 1981, Reagan strode into a joint session of Congress just weeks later – an act that in-and-of-itself boosted America's confidence. He sought immediate action on his economic plan and declared:

> "Our choice is not between a balanced budget and a tax cut . . . by attempting to reduce the deficit through higher taxes, [the budget] will not create the kind of strong economic growth and the new jobs that we must have . . .
>
> Our across-the-board cut in tax rates for a three-year period will give [business] much of the incentive and promise of stability they need to go forward with expansion plans calling for additional employees . . ."

Reagan's words echoed Kennedy's words of two decades earlier. Recall Kennedy's words in response to Eisenhower's recessions:

> "I repeat: our practical choice is not between a tax-cut deficit and budgetary surplus. It is between two kinds of deficits: a chronic deficit of inertia, as the unwanted result of inadequate revenues and a restricted economy; or a temporary deficit of transition, resulting from a *tax cut*

designed to boost the economy, increase tax revenues, and achieve--and I believe this can be done--a budget surplus."

Reagan and Kennedy both faced a stagnant economy and both called for the same remedy: broad, marginal rate tax cuts. It is worthy to note that the marginal tax rate Reagan faced was the same marginal rate that the Kennedy/Johnson tax cuts set: 70%. In other words, in the intervening 20 years, no other President saw the wisdom of the Kennedy cuts and their expanded growth rates. Not coincidentally, three of those Presidents were one-term Presidents or less, the other failed to finish his second term.[24]

There was a reason, of course, that Reagan chose to follow in Kennedy's footsteps and to seek broad tax cuts. For both men, tax cuts represented more than an economic policy. They represented a philosophy that believed in the inspirational power of freedom over the dulling limits of government. They both were policies rooted in *Optimism*

---

[24] It is also worthy to note that Johnson asked for passage of the Kennedy tax cuts after he complained that: "That tax bill has been thoroughly discussed for a year. Now we need action." Reagan's address to the joint session of Congress included a similar complaint: "It's been half a year since the election that charged all of us in this government with the task of restoring our economy . . . Six months is long enough. The American people now want us to act and not in half-measures." Finally, it is also worth considering that both the Kennedy and the Reagan tax cut proposals (a) were both initially met with significant skepticism and (b) were both passed in the wake of assassins' bullets and the sympathetic empowerment they engendered. Would those bills have passed in the absence of those bullets? One can only wonder.

and that *Optimism* ignited our unbound spirits. Such is the power of granting economic freedom and why broad tax cuts are such a winning issue.

A Cocktail Napkin and a Curve

It is worthy to note that the failings of those one-term Presidents did not mean that the effects of the Kennedy tax cuts went unnoticed until Ronald Reagan ran for President. To the contrary, an intellectual movement was brewing from within and without the Republican Party and its story is important for Republicans to understand.

According to some, the take-off point of the movement occurred at dinner in December 1974. Art Laffer was with Donald Rumsfeld, then Chief of Staff to President Gerald Ford, Dick Cheney, then Rumsfeld's deputy, and Jude Wanniski. Art Laffer apparently grabbed a "napkin and a pen and sketched a curve on the napkin illustrating the trade-off between tax rates and tax revenues." [25]

According to Laffer, "Wanniski named the trade-off 'The Laffer Curve.'"[26] Wanniski describes the theory behind the curve as akin to the law of diminishing returns: "Raise tax

---

[25] The Laffer Curve: Past, Present, and Future by Arthur B. Laffer, http://www.heritage.org/Research/Taxes/bg1765.cfm - a definitive article on the Laffer Curve and the effects of tax cuts.

[26] Ibid.

rates too high and commerce will be stifled to the point that tax revenues will decline. At that point a reduction in tax rates will stimulate commerce and revenues will rise."[27]

The prized drawing took this shape:

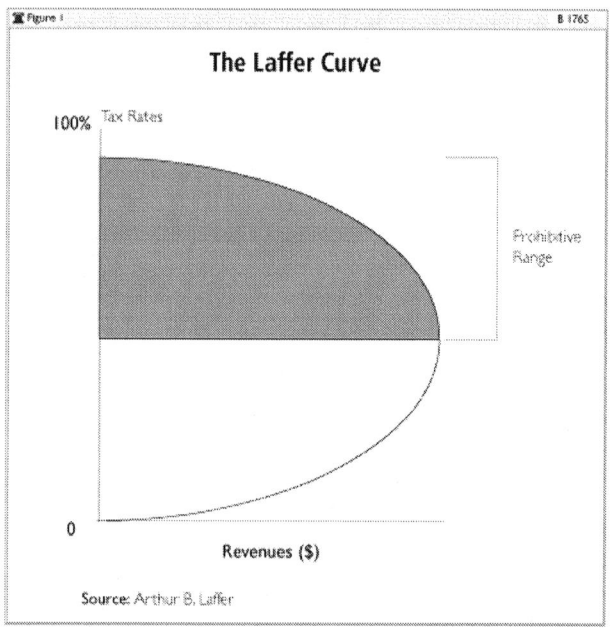

According to Laffer, there is an "economic effect" to cutting taxes, "a *positive* impact that lower tax rates have on work, output, and employment -- and thereby the tax base -- by providing incentives to increase these activities. Raising tax rates has the opposite economic effect by penalizing participation in the taxed activities."[28]

---

[27] The Laffer Curve: Past, Present, and Future by Arthur B. Laffer, http://www.heritage.org/Research/Taxes/bg1765.cfm - a definitive article on the Laffer Curve and the effects of tax cuts.

[28] The Laffer Curve: Past, Present, and Future

Wanniski blamed the woes of the 1970s on rising taxes. He writes that:

"The temporary, but sharp decline of the U.S. economy in the 1970s was the result of the failure of our political leaders to realize the law of diminishing returns was eroding the economy in a new and different way . . .

"We were inflating our way up the progressive tax schedules of the income-tax code. Robert Mundell and Arthur Laffer were the first economists on earth to realize that basic fact and to predict the bad things that followed."[29]

According to Laffer though:

"The Laffer Curve . . . was not invented by me. For example, Ibn Khaldun, a 14th century Muslim philosopher, wrote in his work The Muqaddimah: "It should be known that at the beginning of the dynasty, taxation yields a large revenue from small assessments. At the end of the dynasty, taxation yields a small revenue from large assessments."

Laffer also points to:

"A more recent version (of incredible clarity) was written by John Maynard Keynes:

"Nor should the argument seem strange that taxation may be so high as to defeat its object, and that, given

---

by Arthur B. Laffer, http://www.heritage.org/Research/Taxes/bg1765.cfm - a definitive article on the Laffer Curve and the effects of tax cuts.

[29] SSU Spring Lesson #4: The Laffer Curve, by Jude Wanniski, http://www.wanniski.com/showarticle.asp?articleid=4167

sufficient time to gather the fruits, a reduction of taxation will run a better chance, than an increase, of balancing the budget.

"For to take the opposite view today is to resemble a manufacturer who, running at a loss, decides to raise his price, and when his declining sales increase the loss, wrapping himself in the rectitude of plain arithmetic, decides that prudence requires him to raise the price still more--and who, when at last his account is balanced with nought on both sides, is still found righteously declaring that it would have been the act of a gambler to reduce the price when you were already making a loss."[30]

Regardless of the origin of the curve, even Laffer's critics would come to say that "Professor Laffer is both the creator and the catalyst of the taxpayers' revolt that is sweeping America . . . he is its intellectual leader . . . [and no] serious examination of America's current economic problems, and no significant proposal for tax cuts or tax reform, can fail to include an analysis of the Laffer curve."[31]

Republican appreciation of the Laffer curve, tax cuts and their political/economic implications, however, did not start with Ronald Reagan. That honor belonged, in large

---

[30] The Laffer Curve: Past, Present, and Future by Arthur B. Laffer,
http://www.heritage.org/Research/Taxes/bg1765.cfm referencing John Maynard Keynes, The Collected Writings of John Maynard Keynes (London: Macmillan, Cambridge University Press, 1972).

[31] A Comment on the Laffer Model, Max Moszer,
http://www.cato.org/pubs/journal/cj1n1/cj1n1-2.pdf

degree, to Congressman Jack Kemp and Senator William Roth, who introduced their tax cutting measure in 1977.[32]

According to Bruce Bartlett:

"Kemp and Roth thought that this sharp rise in tax rates [during the '60s and '70s] was largely responsible for the stagnation of the American economy in the 1970s."[33]

Bartlett aptly describes the debate between the emerging pro-growth movement and those inclined to what Kennedy would describe as "intellectual inertia."

"At the time the Kemp-Roth bill was introduced, however, the dominant view among economists was that budget deficits were the primary cause of inflation. They favored tax *increases*, not tax cuts, and said that passage of the Kemp-Roth bill would be dangerously inflationary.

"Kemp and Roth responded that inflation resulted from the Federal Reserve creating too much money,[34] not deficits, and that a tight monetary policy, which they supported, would reduce inflation regardless of how large the deficit was."

---

[32] Kemp-Roth Changed American Economic Policy, Bruce Bartlett, http://www.ncpa.org/edo/bb/2002/bb071502.html.

[33] Kemp-Roth Changed American Economic Policy, Bruce Bartlett, http://www.ncpa.org/edo/bb/2002/bb071502.html. Note that even though tax rates stayed essentially the same, bracket creep pushed the effective tax rates of Americans higher.

[34] A position long championed by the Nobel Prize winning economist Milton Friedman.

"Such a view was absolute heresy in 1977. The Congressional Budget Office, for example, believed that the money supply had nothing whatsoever to do with inflation, and that cutting tax rates would add fuel to it.

"CBO Director Alice Rivlin said that output would fall if tax rates were cut, because workers could work less and still get the same after-tax income."

In my many speeches, exposing that last sentiment garners much amusement. Yet back then, and even today, many on the Left believe it to be so.

History is, however, well aware of with whom Reagan sided in that debate. Indeed, it could be no surprise that Reagan opted for the policy that would have a positive, ***Optimistic*** impact and provide individuals with incentives. Well knowing Supreme Court Chief Justice John Marshall's famous admonition: "The power to tax involves the power to destroy," Reagan "rejected the conventional view and supported Kemp-Roth, making it his principal campaign issue in 1980."[35]

Once elected, on August 13, 1981, Reagan signed into law the Kemp-Roth tax bill which came to be known as the Economic Recovery Tax Act (ERTA). Under the law, marginal income tax rates were reduced by 25 percent over

---

[35] Kemp-Roth Changed American Economic Policy, Bruce Bartlett, http://www.ncpa.org/edo/bb/2002/bb071502.html. Two years prior, the California voters threw down the gauntlet of the tax revolt by passing Prop 13 – a property tax limiting measure that restricted increases in property taxes.

three years and the rates were indexed for inflation to prevent "bracket creep," yet another word that Americans came to know in the late 1970s.[36]

Reagan, Laffer, Kemp & Roth Were Right – Once Again, the Party of *No* Was Wrong

Although the Reagan tax cuts passed, they did so with limited Democrat support. With that historic vote, however, the Republicans and the Democrats had begun the process of role reversal. Recall that Goldwater called the Kennedy tax cuts "gimmickry" and the Republicans thought the cuts, along with the Great Society spending, were reckless. In the early 1980s, the Democrats were against the Reagan tax cuts and claimed that the Reagan military spending was reckless – a complete reversal of roles.

In both cases, the Party that supported tax cuts was right - the Party of *No* was wrong. When Kennedy cut marginal tax rates **for those in the middle and upper brackets, who**

---

[36] The Bracket Creep of the 1970s was a function of rising inflation that pushed wages higher and therefore incomes into higher tax brackets. However, because inflation eroded the value of money and therefore it took more dollars to purchase the same products it did before, people were forced to pay higher taxes without making economic gains. In other words, people were paying higher taxes on higher income but had no greater purchasing power – indeed, many had less because of the higher taxes. Eventually, income taxes were indexed to inflation by Reagan to significantly reduce bracket creep.

can thereby be encouraged to undertake additional efforts and ... invest more capital:

~ The economy grew by 5.8 percent in 1964, and by 6.4 percent in 1965 and 1966, the longest economic expansion to date, and as a result:

~ In the four years following the tax cut, federal government income tax revenue increased by 8.6 percent annually and total government income tax revenue increased by 9.0 percent annually.[37]

~ From 1962-1969, government revenue *increased* 6.4 percent a year, compared with 1.2 percent a year between 1952-1959.

~ Between 1962 and 1969, investment grew at an annual rate of 6.1 percent, far higher than the three percent annual rate for 1959-1962.[38]

Not surprisingly, the Reagan record was similar - despite the much higher hurdle of the more negative effects of stagflation. How damaging was the build up of stagflation from Nixon to Carter? "Over the four years prior to 1983, federal income tax revenue ***declined*** at an average rate of 2.8

---

[37] The Laffer Curve: Past, Present, and Future by Arthur B. Laffer, http://www.heritage.org/Research/Taxes/bg1765.cfm

[38] Do Tax Cuts Effect the Economy? National Center for Policy Analysis, http://taxesandgrowth.ncpa.org/hot_issue/growth/

percent per year, and total government income tax revenue *declined* at an annual rate of 2.6 percent."[39]

The Reagan cuts changed everything:

~ This economic boom lasted 92 months without a recession, from November 1982 to July 1990, the longest period of sustained growth during peacetime and the second-longest period of sustained growth in U.S. history.[40]

~ The average annual growth rate of real gross domestic product (GDP) from 1981 to 1989 *increased* to 3.2 percent per year, compared with 2.8 percent from 1974 to 1981 [Nixon, Ford, Carter] and 2.1 percent from 1989 to 1995 [Bush I, Clinton].[41]

~ Total federal revenues *doubled* from just over $517 billion in 1980 to more than $1 trillion in 1990. In constant

---

[39] The Laffer Curve: Past, Present, and Future by Arthur B. Laffer, http://www.heritage.org/Research/Taxes/bg1765.cfm

[40] The Real Reagan Economic Record: Responsible and Successful Fiscal Policy, by Peter B. Sperry, PhD, http://www.heritage.org/Research/Taxes/BG1414.cfm

[41] Supply Tax Cuts and the Truth About the Reagan Economic Record, by William A. Niskanen and Stephen Moore, http://cato.org/pubs/pas/pa-261.html.

inflation-adjusted dollars, this was a 28 percent increase in revenue.[42]

The Second Part of Reagan's Economic Renewal: Regulatory Reform

If the Democrats under Kennedy and Johnson had a formula for cornering the market on votes during the 1960s, it was by tax cuts and a large scale increase in government handouts. Remember, as you look again at this chart which depicts the gross outlays of federal spending, large scale government was still a new occurrence in the United States when Johnson introduced his Great Society programs. At that time, a politician could sell the notion that government

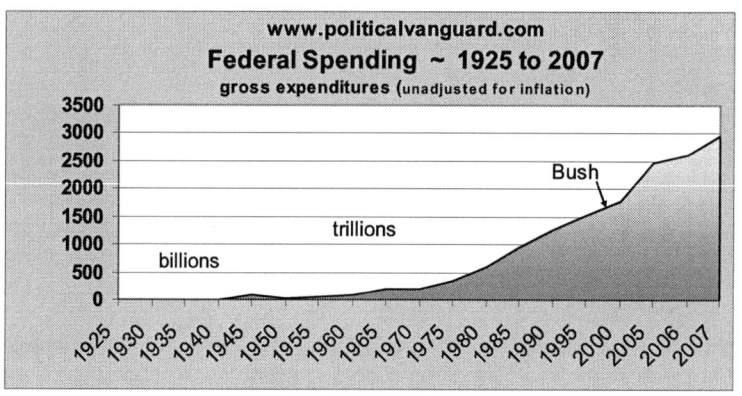

---

[42] The Real Reagan Economic Record: Responsible and Successful Fiscal Policy, by Peter B. Sperry, PhD, http://www.heritage.org/Research/Taxes/BG1414.cfm. Critics will argue that Reagan also raised taxes and those increased tax rates led to more revenues. Without the initial cuts, however, the train would have never started rolling. Further, the higher rates retarded future growth and reduced future tax revenues over time.

was here to help. Not so by Reagan's time.

Indeed, one of Reagan's most memorable lines was: "The nine most terrifying words in the English language are 'I'm here from the government and I'm here to help.'"

Thus, by Reagan's time, although tax cuts were essential to his winning formula, increased government handouts were out of the question. The Reagan answer for the 1980s, and beyond, would be **Government Reform**.

President Reagan made his views on government quite clear in his inaugural address:

"The economic ills we suffer have come upon us over several decades. They will not go away in days, weeks, or months, but they will go away. They will go away because we, as Americans, have the capacity now, as we have had in the past, to do whatever needs to be done to preserve this last and greatest bastion of freedom. **In this present crisis, government is not the solution to our problem. Government is the problem.**"

That was no mere "take away" line in a speech. To the contrary, by saying that, Reagan was signaling a seminal break in philosophy from Presidents Hoover through Carter (excepting only Kennedy). Each of those intervening Presidents grew government or raised tax rates in order to achieve political or social gains – perhaps none more visibly than *Republican* Richard Nixon with his combination of regulation, spending and tax increases. To those Presidents, government was a constructive means to foster social ends and they became the proponents and managers of government.

Reagan had no such ambition. Reagan believed that government was *the* roadblock frustrating desired social gains. Reagan thought that government prevented average citizens from being able to improve their daily lives and the lives of those around them. Government did so by stifling initiative, by wasting resources and through excessive red tape.

So, rather than wanting to manage government, Reagan wanted to change the course of government and inject a bit of freedom into the equation.

As such, faced with a downward spiral of government intervention that left the country in economic trouble, Reagan moved to change the tide. In addition to cutting taxes, if the problem with government was excessive bureaucracy, regulations and their associated costs, what was the rational solution for the "Can Do" Reagan? Simple. Cut regulation, bureaucracy and costs. So, at the very outset of his Administration, President Reagan completely deregulated oil pricing which led to the end of the 1970s oil crisis. Perhaps the most visible step in that regard came in Reagan's first year when Reagan dismissed 13,000 Government Air Traffic Controllers. In early 1982, Reagan called for a New

Federalism – an effort to devolve power away from the federal government down to the states.

In the same year, Reagan established the Grace Commission - announced under the technical name of Private Survey on Cost Control – in an effort to root out government waste. Reagan also took on the third rail of American politics: Social Security. Reagan convened a Blue Ribbon panel headed by Alan Greenspan which resulted in a Social Security Reform bill.

With regard to regulations, under President Reagan, the Office of Management & Budget, or OMB, required strict cost-benefit analyses for all federal regulations. The banking system was deregulated along with the airline industry, the telecommunications industry and the energy industry to name a few – all with considerable Democrat opposition.

Those actions met with varied success but one thing became clear: Republicans became the voice for reform and for cutting red tape. Considerable elements of the Democrat Party, on the other hand, in a preview of the 1990s and early 2000s, fought those reforms at nearly every turn. Consistent with their stance on the Reagan tax cuts, they had become the Party of *No*.

In time, the Republican Party would reap the political gains from that economic growth and reform. For now, however, Reagan turned his attention, the Nation's attention and the World's attention to ending the Cold War.

Reagan Wins The Cold War Through Confidence.

The Cold War long preceded Reagan's tenure in politics – but he was determined that it would not outlast him. In typical Ronald "it can be done" Reagan fashion, when "[a]sked by his first National Security Adviser, Richard Allen, what his Cold War strategy was, Reagan replied: "We win, they lose."[43]

Reagan served clear and plain notice, just months after the passage of his tax bill, that he was not confused as to the state of Cold War affairs. In a speech on November 18, 1981, Reagan laid bare the Soviet actions during the past decade despite America's arm *reductions*:

~ The Soviets steadily increased the number of men under arms. They now number more than double those of the United States.

---

[43] The Gipper's Gift, by: John Wohlstetter, http://www.discovery.org/scripts/viewDB/index.php?command=view&program=Technology%20and%20Democracy&id=2090

~ Over the same period, the Soviets expanded their real military spending by about one-third.

~ The Soviet Union increased its inventory of tanks to some 50,000, compared to our 11,000. Historically a land power, they transformed their navy from a coastal defense force to an open ocean fleet, while the United States, a sea power with transoceanic alliances, cut its fleet in half.

~ During a period when NATO deployed no new intermediate-range nuclear missiles and actually withdrew 1,000 nuclear warheads, the Soviet Union deployed more than 750 nuclear warheads on the new SS-20 missiles alone.

In the face of that build-up, the Left begged the new President to reach a deal with the Soviets. It was the American Left's claim the Soviet build-up was justifiable because of its insecurity brought on by American policies. Such "Blame America First" psychology – if the Soviets are doing something wrong it must be because we were doing something wrong first – would become a staple of the Democrats' Leadership and hasten their Party's reversal of fortune.

Reagan, however, rejected the policies designed to effectuate a draw – such as containment and détente. Instead, Reagan sought to have the West *transcend* the

Soviet Union.[44] In doing so, Reagan adopted an ***Optimistic*** goal for the West to achieve – not the morally "**equivalent**" tie the Left seemed so desperately to want.

According to Newt Gingrich, "the new president set his sights on the *higher goal* of freeing Russia and Eastern European countries from the Communist yoke."

Could Washington and Lincoln be disappointed in such leadership or its theme? Reagan well understood ***Leadership by Higher Purpose*** and couched this battle of the Cold War in moral tones easily appreciated by all but the most hardened. He served notice of that theme in his 1981 Inaugural Speech when he stated:

"Above all, we must realize that no arsenal, or no weapon in the arsenals of the world, is so formidable as the will and moral courage of free men and women. It is a weapon our adversaries in today's world do not have." The next year, speaking to the British Parliament, Reagan predicted that if the Western alliance remained strong it would produce a 'march of freedom and democracy which will leave Marxism-Leninism on the ash heap of history.'"[45]

---

[44] "The West won't contain communism. It will transcend communism. We will dismiss it as some bizarre chapter in human history whose last pages are even now being written." Ronald Reagan 1981.

[45] Russian Revolution, How Reagan won the cold war. by Dinesh D'Souza
http://www.nationalreview.com/flashback/dsouza200406061619.asp [a definitive piece on the subject. Note the similarity in language and theme used by George W. Bush in his second inaugural speech. Dinesh D'Souza can certainly be described as a *New Conservative*.

In other words, Reagan had the temerity to voice what was obvious to all but the Left: that the Soviet system, because it was not based on freedom, was inferior and would therefore eventually fall. It was indeed the Evil Empire – we were not – and good would prevail.

Thus, Reagan had laid out an uplifting vision for the Country and the World. He defined the battle in terms of freedom and democracy versus repression and dictatorship. Now all that was needed were *rational steps* to achieve his *rational goals*.

According to Dinesh D'Souza, a *New Conservative*, "Reagan formulated the notion that the West could use the superior economic resources of a free society to outspend Moscow in the arms race, placing intolerable strains on the Soviet regime."[46]

It also induced thoughtful people like Paul Craig Roberts to state that "Few Americans realize that President Reagan's economic policy won the Cold War by rejuvenating capitalism."[47] Roberts wrote that "Members of the Soviet Academy of Sciences, with whom I spoke in Moscow during the Soviet Union's final months, agreed that it was President

---

[46] Same.

[47] How An Actor Changed The World, Washington Times, June 7, 2004, http://www.washingtontimes.com/commentary/20040606-101646-4699r.htm.

Reagan's **confidence** in capitalism, not his defense buildup that caused Soviet leaders to lose their confidence."

Even so, as D'Souza points out, history recorded Reagan embarked on the largest peace time military buildup on record. It remembers the Reagan Doctrine which challenged the Soviet Union on its fringes by supporting those trying to throw off the Soviet yoke in places near (like Nicaragua) and far (like Cambodia). Reagan even went so far as to tell Gorbachev to his face: "We can . . . continue the arms race, which I think you know you can't win."

In a very real sense the Soviet Union couldn't win that war and Reagan's refusal to give up on SDI was perhaps a final straw in that regard. Not only did the Soviet Union lose its confidence but it also lost the Cold War - an eventuality that Henry Kissinger described as "the most stunning diplomatic feat of the modern era."[48]

Perhaps what is most stunning about the victory was that it was won, as Margaret Thatcher put it, "without firing a shot." In other words, Reagan ended the Third World War, not with a full scale war and all its negative implications, but, instead, by restoring *Optimistic* leadership designed to promote liberty.

In doing so, Reagan could rightfully claim a place alongside America's great Presidents.

---

[48] Russian Revolution, How Reagan won the cold war. by Dinesh D'Souza
http://www.nationalreview.com/flashback/dsouza200406061619.asp

THE THREE PILLARS

"Successful political paradigms coalesce a party's base, attract independents and capitalize on divisions in the opposing party."

Thomas Del Beccaro

As the 1970s came to a close, voters were besieged with poor economic times and high taxes. They were also dispirited at home and with America's standing in the world. By the end of the 1980s, all of that had been reversed. President Reagan, by championing freedom over government intervention, inspired Americans, restored their resolve, purpose and economic prosperity. Along the way, he started a political realignment that lasts to this day. That realignment can be called *The New Conservative Paradigm – a paradigm supported by three Pillars*.

Reagan's pro-growth policies were central to his *Optimism* and his success. They formed the first pillar of *The New Conservative Paradigm*. Prior to Reagan, only Democrat John Kennedy and Republican Calvin Coolidge made dramatic cuts in income taxes and thereby invigorated the Nation. In between, Republicans Hoover, Eisenhower, Nixon, and Ford, along with Democrats Roosevelt, Truman and Carter opted for higher tax rates, slower economies and a less *Optimistic* country.

In making dramatic income tax cuts, Reagan did not simply tell us that lower tax rates spur economic activity. While that is true, it is not an ideal - and while it makes good policy, it does not inspire generations to greater achievements - which inspiration is the responsibility of leadership.

Instead, Reagan had a *Higher Purpose* – he sided with the potential of the individual over the false promise of government. The magnitude of that change in governmental philosophy, and its effect today, cannot be overstated – and within that explanation lays the political power of **Pillar Number One**.

During the 1960s, when the Democrats were winning votes with programs, the average person believed that government programs could well be a force for good – and so Johnson, Nixon, Ford and Carter ballooned government programs hoping for political success. By Reagan's time, however, the empty promises of government programs had been exposed and the reach of government had simply gone too far. Reagan tapped into the river of anxiety and frustration amongst the electorate that government, with its regulations and mandates, was an impediment to the ability of families and individuals to succeed.

Americans saw Reagan take on government and by doing so they felt he was restoring freedom to them. In a very real way, that is what **Pillar Number One** is all about. It is not merely some mathematical policy of lowering tax rates for which lip service need be paid. It is a liberating force because it ennobles the needs of individuals and families over government and recognizes the power of opportunity over the shackles of government dependency.

In becoming its champion, Reagan demonstrated his understanding of what President Coolidge said so long ago that the "wise and correct course to follow in taxation is not to destroy those who have already secured success, but to create conditions under which everyone will have a better chance to be successful."

Reagan's policies were also in keeping with Chief Justice John Marshall's telling words that "in a free government, almost all other rights would become worthless if the government possessed power over the private fortune of every citizen."

In other words, **Pillar Number One is nearly synonymous with freedom itself and** its advocates are guardians of our freedoms. It is also plainly a policy of **Optimism** and a policy that inspires greater achievement.

Contrast that, if you will, with the *constant, negative* drum beat of Democrat leaders to raise taxes – a policy that outright advocates *punishing* those that succeed and a policy that limits freedom. "Give me your vote and then we will take your money" – such is their demand. It is hardly the stuff of leadership and certainly not inspiring. Indeed, rare is a time when government programs (other than perhaps war efforts) inspire a people to higher achievement. Such inspiration is only the domain of *Liberty* – an idea whose sworn adversary is government.

As a political matter, by the time Reagan got his tax cuts, he had coalesced Republicans behind his program. Many Independents supported his call to end bracket creep and to turn the economy around. The Democrats, for their part, were divided on the issue. By the end of the 1980s, and the 92 straight months of economic expansion, tax cuts were a powerful economic and successful political strategy that coalesced the Republican Party, attracted Independents and capitalized on the division within the Democrat Party.

In other words, Reagan's use of **Pillar Number One** was a success economically, politically and historically.

Pillar Number One, of Reagan's *New Conservative Paradigm,* was not without companions. Reagan exuded, if not personified, two other important characteristics that would play a key role in the construction of *The New Conservative Paradigm*. In what would become **Pillar Number Two**, in contrast to the Democrats' growing self-doubt about America, Ronald Reagan unabashedly believed in America, its purpose and its defense. **Pillar Number Three** would become Reagan's counter to the Left's social revolutions: his Respect for American Traditions and Values. All were welcome tonics to a nation wearied by the counter-culture years.

In doing so, President Reagan not only gave greater impetus to the emerging *New Conservative Paradigm*, but he also vanquished the negative vocabulary we came to know in the Carter years. President Reagan even engendered a new phrase of his own – The Reagan Democrat – and with that, the reversal in party fortunes drew closer.

Democrats Lend A Helping Hand with Pillar Number Two
The Anti – "American Power" Wing Takes Hold

President Reagan believed in America, its purpose and its defense. He took pride in America and her traditions. Those beliefs were essential to defeating the defeatists of the prior four years. The Democrats, however, were not always defeatists.

To the contrary, Reagan's beliefs were not unlike President Kennedy's. He did not doubt America or its purpose or its defense. In fact, Kennedy still wanted the US to be the world's "arsenal of democracy." Kennedy sought "not merely peace for Americans but peace for all men and women -- not merely peace in our time but peace in all time." Kennedy's obvious reference to the mistaken pacifist Chamberlain, who had declared "peace in our time" in reference to his meeting with Hitler just before World War II, made it very clear that his was an America of strength and purpose – a marked contrast to today's Democrat leadership and the Left in general. Indeed, Kennedy, as indicated by his authorization of the Bay of Pigs operation (his attempt to topple Castro), proved he was prepared to fight preemptively for freedom. Modern Democrat leaders, by contrast, seek immediate withdrawal from Iraq and other places.

Kennedy's themes, in that regard, were traditional American themes. They were a proud heritage for a Country that had liberated Europe twice and South Korea within the previous forty-five years – a heritage celebrated by Kennedy and the Democrats when they had huge majorities in Congress.

With the loss of Kennedy, however, the tone of the Democrat Party changed dramatically as the 1960s progressed. In an ever so brief period of time, the Democrat Party became more than suspicious of American power and nearly contemptuous of its nature.

The obvious backdrop of the times was the Vietnam War. That War turned the Democrat Party, the Left, and the Media four square against the use of American power. The irony of that, of course, is that the Vietnam War was not fully engaged until Democrats Kennedy and Johnson made it so. Keep in mind that President Johnson "Americanized" the Vietnam War just three years earlier, in 1965, when he committed 90,000 troops to defeating the North Vietnamese.

The Presidential election of 1968 placed that new-found anti-American power bias on display in front of a wide television audience. A year before the November election, an anti-war Senator named Eugene McCarthy of Minnesota announced he would run for President against a sitting pro-war incumbent, President Johnson. His remarkable success against Johnson, in the March 1968 New Hampshire primary, directly led to Johnson withdrawing from the 1968 Presidential race on the last day of March, 1968.

Just before that, Senator Robert Kennedy joined the race for the White House on the Democrats side. Soon thereafter, Vice President Hubert Humphrey also joined the race. Kennedy and McCarthy were supported by anti-war protestors they actively cultivated.

As the anti-war fever of their Party grew to a pitch, the Democrats' convention in Chicago was marred by violent anti-war protests in August of 1968. The Nation, Democrats included, was taken aback. Hubert Humphrey became the Democrats nominee at that convention and in deference to the strength of the anti-wars Democrats, one month before the election; Humphrey took the position that the Vietnam War had to end. He did so without an assurance that the US would complete its mission.[49]

The antiwar movement culminated in some respects just four days before the election. In what appeared to be a concession to the anti-war movement that gripped his Party, President Johnson announced the suspension of the bombing of North Vietnam.

---

[49] Much like the position many Democrats took on Iraq in the run up to the 2004, 2006 and 2008 elections.

Four days later, Republican Richard Nixon completed his political comeback by defeating Democrat Hubert Humphrey.

In rather simple terms, the Democrats lost that election more than the Republican Nixon won that election. Remember that the Republicans were not offering a domestic agenda much different from that of the Democrats. The Republicans believed in tax increases and spending as did the Democrats. However, the Democrats, in a very short period of time and in a very public and startling way, tore their party asunder over **Pillar Number Two**: *Belief in America and her Defense*. They went from the pro-war establishment party to a divided anti-war party. It proved too much for voters to understand, let alone support, in sufficient numbers. As a result, the relatively unified Republicans, with the help of Independents, defeated those war-divided Democrats – just as they did in 1860 when the Democrats were divided over the Civil War and a relatively united Republican Party won. In that way, the election of 1968 proved the paradigm that "Successful political paradigms coalesce a party's base, attract independents and capitalize on divisions in the opposing party."

The anti-war conversion was a remarkable turn around for the Democrats and the Left. After all, the Bay of Pigs took place under the watchful eye of the Kennedy

Administration just seven and one half years before. Again, President Johnson "Americanized" the Vietnam War just three years earlier. Even the *New York Times,* in 1961, supported the use of American force in an editorial that:

" . . . spoke of "communist aggression" against South Vietnam that had been "launched as a calculated and deliberate operation by the Communist leaders of the North." The editorial continued: "The outlook in South Vietnam certainly gives no basis for optimism . . . *Free World* forces, however, still have a chance in South Vietnam, and *every effort should be made the save the situation.*"[50]

Those lost echoes seem more than long ago and far away. They also were the last time the Democrat Party was ahead on **Pillar Number Two**.

To Mona Charen, a **New Conservative**, "[t]he Leftist critique of America's role in Vietnam set the tone for every Cold War debate that would follow for the next thirty-five years."[51]

Charen believes that:

"The Left's explanation of America's participation in the war was cartoonish and grotesque. It featured the U.S. in the role of international outlaw, interfering in a civil war for the

---

[50] *Useful Idiots,* by Mona Charen, p. 25, citing Norman Podhoretz' work, *Why We Were In Vietnam.* Useful Idiot's is a remarkable book for anyone interested in an exhaustive history of Left's emerging and enduring "Blame America First" mentality.

[51] Id. at 28.

sole purpose of propping up a corrupt dictatorship that would do its bidding. Some radicals went further, arguing that the U.S. had sent troops ten thousand miles across the globe to secure mineral rights . . . for large American Corporations . . . [or that] the true reason for American intervention was 'to serve the economic interests of American businessman . . . [and] they painted the North Vietnamese and Vietcong as our victims.'"[52]

If you read that again, you can hear in those words a mantra repeated over and over again by the Left, and leading Democrats, whenever and wherever the US projected force abroad – whether it was in El Salvador, Nicaragua, Grenada, or in Iraq. No matter what the stakes, no matter what the nature of the enemy, a strong element of the Democrat Party was bound and determined to Blame America First.[53] And if America was to blame, the way to curb the appetite of the "military industrial complex" was to cut its funding.

In 1968, that mentality created an opening for the Republican Party to demonstrate that it was better suited to defend America – an opening not many years removed from when Lyndon Johnson used a "mushroom cloud" campaign ad to convince many Americans that Republicans and their Candidate Barry Goldwater were too dangerous to be trusted

---

[52] *Useful Idiots*, by Mona Charen, p. 28.

[53] It was a tone that stayed with a considerable wing of the Democrats that found voice once again in 2004 in Howard Dean. It was also on awkward display when John Kerry paraded Vietnam vets in front of the camera as part of his 2004 acceptance speech.

with the defense of America. Nixon, despite his shortcomings, exploited that opening to win the 1968 election.

Between 1968 and 1980, the succession of Democrat Leaders which included McGovern and Carter did little to change their new identity with respect to **Pillar Number Two**. In 1980, after the failures of Carter, Candidate and President Ronald Reagan seized upon that opening again to his and our great success. As we saw in the previous Chapters, Reagan embraced America's historic ideals as expressed by Washington and Lincoln. Simply stated, Reagan whole-heartedly believed that America had a **Higher Purpose** and there was nothing for which America had to be ashamed. To the contrary, in full patriotic fashion, for Reagan America was a "shining city on the hill." Two large electoral victories appear to have demonstrated which view Americans preferred between the Democrats' self-blame and Reagan's pride.

That **Blame America First** mentality, however, was not the only turn against traditional America that the Democrats took in the lead up to the Reagan years.

The Anti – "American Tradition" Wing Takes Hold

To the extent that a considerable wing of the Democrat Party would become identified as anti-American Power during the 1960s and 1970s, other and similar elements of their Party took on traditional American life.

Note that prior to the Reagan and the Reagan Democrat, it was no secret of American politics that the Democrat Party was perceived as the champion of the working man, blue collar families and minorities. It was a perception long cultivated by a Party that called Franklin Delano Roosevelt its own and was the forerunner of ***Pillar Number Three, Respect for American Traditions & Values***.

That perception can be traced in large part to the Great Depression era - if not before. Many in America were convinced that the Great Depression was the fault of Capitalists and their playground of Big Business. It was also thought that Big Business was the domain of Country-Club Republicans and their Party – a holdover from the days of Rockefeller and the industrial titans.

We know now that the cause of Great Depression was not Big Business but ineffective Big Government. In the lead up to the worst of the Great Depression, the Federal Reserve allowed the money supply to shrink by nearly 1/3 and the Congress did its part by enacting trade killing tariffs known as the Smoot-Hawley Act, and, of course, raising marginal tax rates.[54] Those acts, and others, turned a significant recession into the Great Depression.

---

[54] Congress also raised the top marginal income-tax rate from 24 percent to 63 percent after President Hoover persuaded them that "nothing is

Nevertheless, at the time, and for years later, it was perceived as a result of the failings of Capitalism not the failings of Government – failings which occurred on the watch of *Republican* Herbert Hoover. Given those perceptions, under a Democrat FDR, the national response to the Great Depression was not less government interference but, instead, more government interference.

The succeeding forty years reinforced those perceptions for many. They became a history whereby the Democrat Party purchased the loyalty of the less fortunate with a series of New Deals, Wars on Poverty and Great Societies. As we have seen, the Republican Party had no similar, or more importantly, *rival* agenda or theme with which to court the working class electorate. That changed under Reagan but not without significant help from the Left and their party, the Democrats.

~ ~ ~ ~

As we review this history, we would do well to remember the following from American historian Will Durant. He surmised that tradition is to the civilization what memory is to the individual. If the individual loses his

---

more necessary at this time than balancing the budget." As for the shrinking money supply, imagine if nearly 1/3 of your assets or income suddenly were gone. Would you cut back on your spending? Perhaps decidedly so? The America of the '30s certainly answered that question decidedly so and many lost their jobs and had little to no money to spend.

memory - he is lost, so too for civilizations that discard their traditions too quickly - the American civilization included. For much of America, that is the crux of the matter. The pace and nature of the social change pushed by the Left is too much for their sensibilities – especially when the Left demands more than tolerance – they also want Americans to change their lifestyle, their school books and often times their most cherished beliefs. Such demands are not easily met socially or politically.

So, as the American standard of living rose during the '60s, '70s and '80s, and families lessened their concern with economic issues and increased their concern with social stability, Middle America began to strike back. Indeed, as our "Rosie The Riveter" and "Father Knows Best" idealism was replaced with "Anti-War Protests" and "Archie Bunker," the American Left, and the Democrat leaders that pander to them, caused a majority of Americans to recoil; to seek refuge for the dizzying pace of change – and to identify with a party and a leader that respected America, her traditions and values.

It was not an unnatural reaction. Often in history, when the traditions of a group are threatened, the group reacts by closing ranks and clutching ever tighter to their customs and beliefs – just like individuals who become defensive when they are challenged or criticized. Such is the history of the last 40 years for many Americans and the dynamic that would lead to Republicans taking a lead on **Pillar Number Three,** *Respect for American Traditions & Values*.

Thus, although the media would have Americans believe otherwise, it can be fairly said that the Republican Party did not start a religious uprising to do battle with the Left. Nor did the Religious Right seek the battle that ensued. The awakening of the so-called Religious Right, in fact, was instigated by the Left which was far too antagonist and disrespectful to many Americans and their traditions. The Republican Party became the natural home to many of those people motivated by a desire to hold on to their beliefs and their traditions – which was no small incentive. Much of Reagan's success can be credited to the fact that he understood that dynamic and then worked with them to channel that motivation into a political force. Indeed, rather than threatening American traditions, Reagan respected them and publicly stood proudly by them.

In doing so, Reagan provided calm amongst the social storm on the Left. To this day, the Republicans benefit from that leadership in the form of increased vote totals and so many grassroots volunteers – all of which translates into a lead with respect to *Pillar Number Three, Respect for American Traditions & Values.* For their part, the Far Left continues to push the envelope further and further. Amidst such social arrogance, the Republicans can stay ahead if they continue to honor American values and traditions and if they remain the calm amidst the Left's social storm.

~ ~ ~

Most prominent in that agenda was the Left's desire to remove God from the Public Square – a predilection that struck at the hearts and imaginations of many Americans. And contrary to most American's understanding, it was a rather recent phenomenon.

As a practical matter, prior to FDR and his Supreme Court Packing Plan, the Federal Government was simply not that large or that active. The States were the primary crucible of legislative and judicial action. FDR's New Deal, however, ballooned the size of the Federal Government. A suddenly larger Federal Government proceeded to grab power from the States on a variety of levels. In order to achieve those goals, Roosevelt devised his Court Packing Plan as a prelude to a power grab by the federal courts.[55]

---

[55] In 1937, after the Supreme Court struck down several key provisions of Roosevelt's New Deal, Roosevelt proposed expanding the Court from nine Justices to fifteen and forcing the retirement of Justices at age 70. It was an obvious ploy for Roosevelt to appoint judges who would support his expansion of federal power. In the face of that Roosevelt's plan, two Justices switched their votes and paved the way for Roosevelt's New Deal expansion of Federal Power. It must be noted that the rapidly expanding power of the federal judiciary was the realization of Thomas Jefferson's fear expressed by him in this quote: "The great object of my fear is the federal judiciary. That body, like Gravity, ever acting, with noiseless foot, & unalarming advance, gaining ground step by step, and holding what it gains, is ingulphing insidiously the special governments [i.e. the states] into the jaws of that which feeds them."

Although Roosevelt was primarily concerned with expanding the power of the federal government over economic and regulatory issues, in time, the Left, and the Democrat Party in particular, would use the expanding powers of the federal courts to advocate social changes.

As part of that dynamic, issues we previously understood as "social issues" subject to social norms across a varied Nation were being "decided" by Federal courts. Lawsuits proliferated claiming that the acts occurring within a single state violated the US Constitution to the alleged detriment of everyone. In that train arrived a series of Separation of Church and State/Establishment Clause cases heard in the Federal Courts. Many of those cases were driven by an express desire on the part of the Left to have public expressions of our religious culture, if not our history, stricken from the Public Square.

Of course, it is the belief of most Americans, however misguided, that the Founders erected the proverbial "wall" known as the Separation between Church and State. It is also widely assumed that that principle was preserved by our Court system throughout our history. Honest history books, however, give a rather different account.

In fact, only *two* cases in the 150 years prior to FDR cited that notion of a separation between Church & State[56] –

---

[56] That fact and others like them are cited in an exhaustive history of this topic written by David Barton in his work ***Original Intent, The Courts, the Constitution & Religion.***

one to uphold a law against polygamy in response to the polygamist's defense of a so-called religious right to do so[57] - and the other striking down an Oregon law that would have required all children to attend public school.[58] Neither case could be characterized as anti-religious: the former striking down polygamy and the latter actually *preserving* the right of parents to send their children to *religious* schools.

Thus, for over 150 years, the Federal Courts left alone our religious heritage if not supported it. Why? Although too voluminous of a topic to adequately handle in this book, in all likelihood it was because our cultural heritage of expressions of God in the Public Square were countless if not ubiquitous – they were an integral part of our culture. They stemmed from the very birth of the First Amendment and, despite being under fire, they last until this day. Consider if you will that:

"On the *same day* that Congress approved of the final wording of the First Amendment to the Constitution (Congress shall make no law respecting an establishment of religion or prohibiting the free exercise thereof), that same Congress passed a resolution "to wait upon the President of the United States to request that he would recommend to the people of the United States a day of public thanksgiving and *prayer, to be observed by acknowledging with grateful*

---

[57] Reynolds v. United States, 98 U.S. 145 (1878).

[58] Pierce v. Society of Sisters, 268 U.S. 510 (1923).

hearts the many signal favors of the Almighty God." 8 days later, Washington issued a proclamation that began *"Whereas it is the duty of all nations to acknowledge the providence of almighty God."*[59]

Regardless of what you may have thought before, it is beyond reason to believe that the Founders expected the Federal Government to root out God from the Public Square by approving of a provision "acknowledging . . . Almighty God" and a day of national prayer on the *same day* that they approved of the 1st Amendment.

The following historical facts strengthen that analysis:

~ The first Supreme Court Justice John Jay, in response to a request about whether clergymen could attend regional functions of the Supreme Court wrote: "The custom in New England of clergyman's attending should in my opinion be observed and continued."[60]

~ In 1800, the US Congress authorized the Capitol to be used as a Church building and three years later John Quincy Adams confirmed his attendance to such proceedings in his diary.[61]

~ When the Capitol was rebuilt, after the British burned it in 1814, in the House chambers a series of reliefs were

---

[59] ***Original Intent, The Courts, the Constitution & Religion*** by David Barton

[60] Id.

[61] Id.

placed on the walls around the entire chamber. All of the reliefs were profiles except one: the relief that directly faces the podium - from which the State of the Union is given. Whose relief looks directly upon the legislators as they deliberate? Moses.

~ In 1864, so many years after the First Amendment was adopted, the phrase "In God We Trust" first started appearing on US currency after an act of Congress that year – a practice which continues to this day.

The state courts acted in concert with those traditions. Consider this passage from *Religion in the United States of America*, Rev. R. Baird, 1844, Blackie and Son, Publishers, p. 275, about an 1812 criminal case:

"A person was indicted at New York . . . for aspersing the character of Jesus Christ, and denying the legitimacy of his birth. He was tried, condemned, fined, and imprisoned. On that trial chief Justice Kent, still living, and thought second to none in the country in point of legal knowledge, expressed himself as follows:

"The people of this state, in common with the people of this country, profess the general doctrines of Christianity as the rule of their faith and practice; and to scandalize the Author of these doctrines is not only, in a religious point of view, extremely impious, but, even in respect to the obligation due to society, is a gross violation of decency and good order.

"Nothing could be more offensive to the virtuous part of the community, or more injurious to the tender morals of the young, than to declare such profanity lawful.

"It would go to confound all distinction between things sacred and profane . . . No government . . .among any of the polished nations of antiquity, and none of the institutions of modern Europe (a single minority case excepted), ever hazard such a bold experiment upon the solidity of the public morals, as to permit with impunity, and under the sanction of their tribunals, the general religion of the community to be openly insulted and defamed . . .

"True, the constitution has discarded religious establishments. It does not forbid judicial cognizance of those offenses against religion and morality which have no reference to any such establishment, or to any particular form of government, but are punishable because they strike at the root of moral obligation, and weaken the security of the social ties.

"To construe it as breaking down the common-law barriers against licentious, wanton, and impious attacks upon Christianity itself, would be an enormous perversion of its meaning."

How could a judge, claimed by at least one to be *"second to none in the country in point of legal knowledge,"* render such a decision over 20 years after the passage of the First Amendment to the Constitution? Quite simply, because it was in keeping with the America culture, then and even now.

It was that tradition the Left took on with a series of cases that struck at the heart of America's religious heritage. As David Barton points out, the assault has been relentless:

~ numerous cases in the 1960s and 1970s against prayer in school,

~ a 1965 case holding that freedom of speech was guaranteed to students unless the topic is religious,

~ a 1976 case holding that it was unconstitutional for a Board of Education to use or refer to the word "God,"

~ a 1979 case holding that it was unconstitutional for a kindergarten teacher to ask whose birthday is celebrated by Christmas.[62]

Quite simply, if it was not unconstitutional for church services to be held in the US Capitol, in what sense is it unconstitutional for prayer to occur in a school? If Washington, who knew something of the founding of our Country, could establish a day of Thanksgiving to the Almighty God, in what sense was it unconstitutional for a public official to refer to the word God?

For many Americans then, and now, there simply was no logical answer to those questions and others like them. In response to years of such legalistic and other attacks on their way of life, if not their heritage, significant parts of the Country, including those so pejoratively referred to by the Media as being in the Bible Belt, took considerable offense, mobilized and became the Religious Right.

---

[62] ***Original Intent, The Courts, the Constitution & Religion*** by David Barton

Candidate Ronald Reagan agreed with them and the Democrat's once Solid South, populated with Evangelical Christians, agreed with him. In the 1980 general election, Republican Ronald Reagan carried the South (excluding Georgia). It would soon become the Solid Republican South that it is today. But that was not all.

Though it had attacked America's history as a liberator and its religious traditions, the Left was not yet finished. The social fabric of America was stretched to the point of tearing, on a number of other issues as well, leading up to Reagan's election and beyond.

The Left's and the Democrat's favorite method for change seemed to become lawsuits. Unhappy with the pace of "progress" afforded them by legislators and Presidents, let alone ever emancipating technology, lawsuits were used to secure "rights."

Civil rights cases abounded and the case that changed the Unites States forever was *Griswold v. Connecticut* - a case decided in 1965 by the U.S. Supreme Court. It established a "zone of privacy" that was hitherto unknown. In time, that "zone of privacy" would lead to perhaps the most famous Supreme Court decision of the latter half of the 20th Century: *Roe v. Wade*. That case too recognized a Federal "right" that superseded "rights" not given in certain states. And with that case, the issue of Life was thrust with great verve square and center into American public life.

For many in the Country, the dizzying pace of the 1960s was simply too much for the small town ideal to which they held. The 1970s & 1980s, filled with MTV, "R" rated movies, teen pregnancies and the like provided them little in the way of relief. Although the American historical philosophers Will and Ariel Durant could leisurely question whether:

> "The moral laxity of our times is a herald of decay rather than a painful or delightful transition between a moral code that has lost its agricultural basis and another that our industrial civilization has yet to forge into social order and normality . . .[63]

For many Americans, whose simple ambition was to have their children's childhood to be as innocent as theirs, the assault on their sensibilities and values was simply too much – and played no small role in the rise of the Religious Right – a political force that cemented **Pillar Number Three,** *Respect for American Traditions & Values* in Reagan's favor.

Indeed, the candidate and then President Ronald Reagan alternatively fostered and echoed their sentiment. Quite simply, amidst such turmoil and moral relevativeness, he represented a nostalgic view of America – one of strength and honor.

---

[63] The Lessons of History, Will & Ariel Durant.

Put another way, President Reagan, and in time, the Republican Party, in addition to its pro-growth policies, became the political protectors of God and Country. That dynamic also marked the evolution of *Pillar Number Three* from concern for working families to the preservation of the traditional ideals and values cherished by Middle America. The Democrats, along with their counterparts in Hollywood and the Media completed the 1980s with a disdain for such concepts.

Nearly a quarter century later, in the form of NASCAR Dads, the Evangelical vote, the transitioning Catholic vote and more, the reversal in fortunes for the Parties on **Pillar Number Three**, *Respect for American Traditions & Values*, remains prevalent. It speaks to many soccer moms and families now concerned with social stability - and is no small key to *The New Conservative Paradigm*.

Taking Stock ~ Part II

We have now progressed through the 1970s and into the late 1980s. The reversal in fortunes of the parties on issues was nearly complete and the Republican majority would not be far off.

Before we move on, let us briefly revisit our chart from before and rename a segment to incorporate our new understanding of Democrats disarray in the late 1960s. Surely the factors that persuaded Johnson's decision not to seek re-election caused great difficulty for his Party. Amidst the Vietnam War, divisions in his Party abounded. The Republicans were certainly able to capitalize on that dynamic. But as we have seen, for the first time, and in a fashion dramatically different from Kennedy, the Democrats turned against America, its ideals and some of its traditions. The intensity of that turn at least partially explains how the Democrats lost the White House – along with their Party divisions and their abandonment of pro-growth ideals.

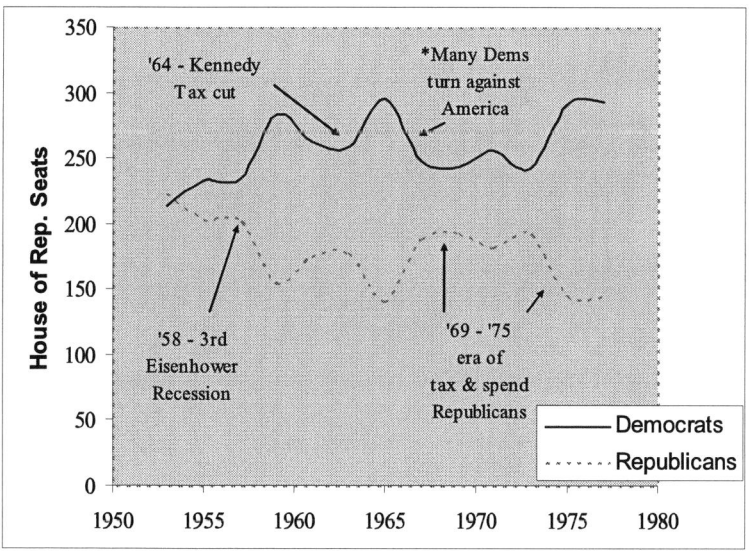

In the prelude to the Nixon Election in late 1968, we can see now that the Democrat Party no longer spoke of tax cuts or growth. To the contrary, the election was fought on the issue of the war and many Democrats spoke out virulently against America and its values. That produced an opening for Republicans. Although the Republicans became the Party identified with a strong national defense, unfortunately Republicans did not grab the pro-growth mantle. As a result, neither Nixon nor Ford were celebrated for their economic policies.

As we have seen, those failings led to Carter. Reagan, however, truly began the process of making the Republican Party the Majority Party.

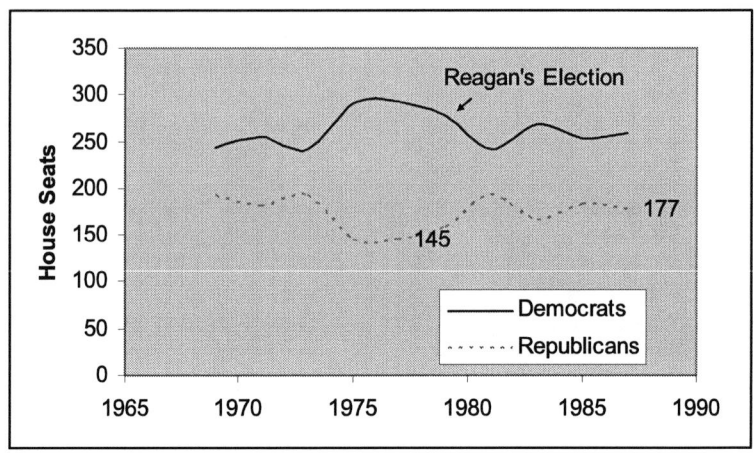

Under President Reagan, the Republicans narrowed the gap in Congress. The party recovered from their low of 145 seats in the House. They reached a high of 192 seats with his first election but fell back 10 seats with the difficulties of Iran-Contra and after *raising* taxes in 1985.

Under Reagan, the Republican Party actually became the majority Party in the Senate for the first time since 1953 - before the Iran-Contra affair and a series of non-income tax increases[64] would cost Republicans their majority.

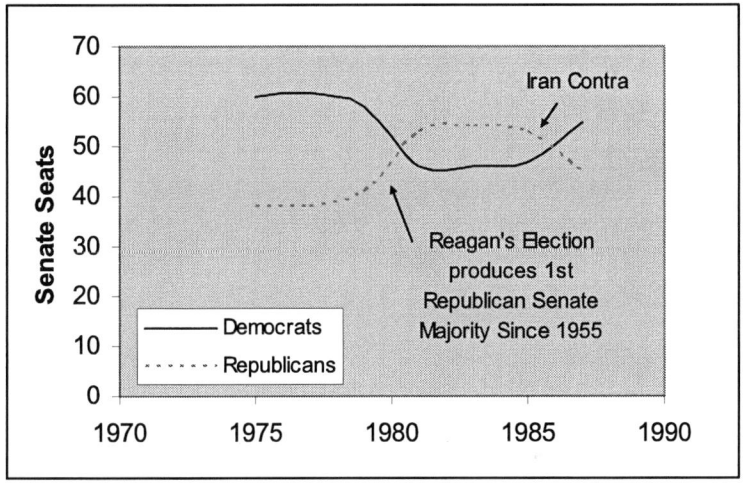

However, under Reagan, the parties had largely reversed their roles.

The Republicans now stood for what would become *The New Conservative Paradigm*:

---

[64] In 1983, Reagan agreed to raise the Social Security tax rate. In 1984, Reagan raised taxes again by signing the Deficit Reduction Act of 1984. Those increases, and others that were passed – and the negative drag on the economy associated with them, did not come close to offset the benefits of the income tax reductions over time and were not helpful politically.

~ Pillar Number One: Pro- Growth Policies including cutting taxes

~ Pillar Number Two: Belief in America, its purpose and its defense, and

~ Pillar Number Three: Respect for American Traditions and Values

All of those positions could rightfully be identified with John F. Kennedy during the early 1960s and produced considerable majorities for the Democrats in the early and mid 1960s.

The Democrat Leaders, on the other hand, in the late 1980s stood for:

~ Raising taxes

~ Skepticism of America and weak on defense, and

~ Callousness, if not contempt, towards America's Traditional Ideals and Values

The first of those current Democrat positions, raising taxes, could more or less be identified with the Republicans in the early and mid 1960s. As we saw, Republicans opposed the Kennedy tax cuts and the Democrats were therefore ahead on *Pillar Number One*. As to defense, Johnson successfully painted the Republicans as untrustworthy leaving the Democrats ahead on *Pillar Number Two*. And, as we have seen, dating back to the New

Deal if not beyond, the Democrats, up until Reagan, had a stronger hold on *Pillar Number Three*: concern for the working family.

Reagan reversed all of that. However, the next two US Presidents failed to heed any of Kennedy's or Reagan's lessons. As a result, one became a one-term President and the other, despite his tri-angulations, would cause his Party to endure unprecedented losses in Congress – such are the stories of the first President Bush and William Jefferson Clinton.

BUSH 41 CLINTON THE YEARS OF LOST OPPORTUNITY

> "He who refuses to embrace a unique opportunity loses the prize as surely as if he had failed."
> **William James**

The enormous success of the Reagan Presidency was not without its legacies. America and its economy recovered. The end of the Cold War was near. Tax cuts became more than a policy tool, they became an inspirational force and the new fault line in American politics. Party affiliation began to change along with the balance of power in Congress.

The Presidencies of George Herbert Walker Bush and Bill Clinton, however, seemed to ignore the lessons of the past. As a result, both Presidencies represent missed opportunities for their Parties.

As a statistical matter, we can see that the Presidency of George Herbert Walker Bush, or Bush 41, did little to improve the Republican fortunes in Congress. The Presidency of Bill Clinton, on the other hand, did great things for Republicans.

The Bush 41 & Clinton Years

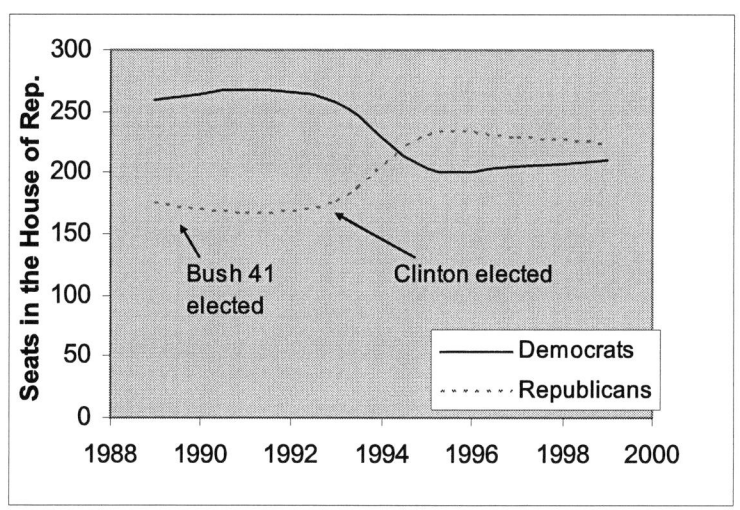

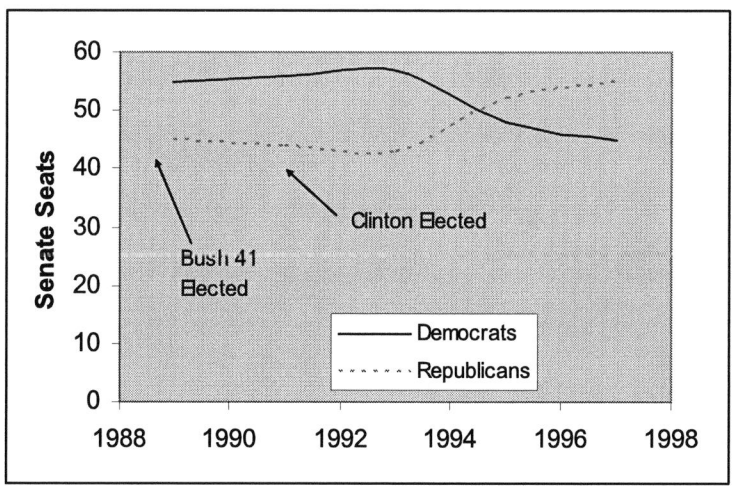

Conventional wisdom, of course, would lead us to believe that the Presidency of Bush 41 should have led to more Republicans in Congress and the Presidency of President Bill Clinton should have led to more Democrats.

Why they did not was just one more step towards the cementing of *The New Conservative Paradigm*.

The Factors That Were Constant

Of the Pillars we are following 1) Pro-growth Policies, 2) Belief in America, it Purpose and its Defense, and 3) Respect for American Ideals and Values, the latter two changed little during the Bush 41/Clinton years. If anything, they became more deep-seated.

Bush 41 Maintains The Republican Lead on Pillar Number Two

By all accounts, it must be said that the successes of Bush 41 were not in the economic arena but in the area of national defense and foreign policy. Bush 41 undertook many and varied actions that cemented the Republican Party's image as strong on defense.

1989
~ Bush offers assistance to Poles in their election that ends the one-party Communist rule.
~ Bush announces restrictions on China in response to the Tiananmen Square Crisis.

~ The Berlin Wall falls and Bush meets Gorbachev in Malta

~ Bush removes Dictator Noriega from Panama

1990

~ Bush signs Arms Reduction Agreement with Russia

~ Bush sends troops to Middle East in response to Iraqi invasion of Kuwait

1991

~ Operation Desert Storm frees Kuwait from Saddam Hussein.

~ Bush signs Start I with Gorbachev

~ The Soviet Union Dissolves

1992

~ Bush and Yeltsin declare an end to the Cold War and agree to reduce nuclear stock piles

~ Bush signs arms treaties with the new Russian Republics

Few four-year periods in America History or World History could boast such successes. The fall of the Berlin Wall was a most demonstrable end to an era. The Republicans rightfully claimed and were given credit for winning the Cold War.⁶⁵ Beyond that, the diplomatic run up to Operation Desert Storm was a significant achievement during Bush 41's Presidency – *except at home with Democrats of course.*

The Democrat Leadership Cements Their Weak Defense Credentials

We can recall that when the Republicans were faced with the Kennedy/ Johnson tax cuts in 1964, Republicans had a choice to either be *right* or to be *contrary*. They chose contrary and paid for that in Congressional elections for years. When it came to liberating Kuwait, the Democrats also chose to be contrary and pay for that decision to this day.

When Iraq invaded Kuwait, the Democrats held a majority in the US Senate by a margin of 55 – 45. The vast majority of those Democrats, 45, voted **against** Operation Desert Storm. According to Senator Robert Dole, "Desert Storm's defeat in the U.S. Senate would have been one of history's most serious blows against a President in a crisis."⁶⁶

---

[65] Despite such recognition, President Bush missed an opportunity to highlight the fall of the Berlin Wall – choosing instead to say we do not want to "gloat." It is a reluctance his son George W. Bush shares given his refusal to tout the successes of his own Presidency.

[66] The Tough Choices, Robert Dole's Wall Street Journal from March 13, 2001

Nevertheless, the voices of the Senate Democrats confirmed that for many, the Democrat Party was little changed from 1968. As you read these quotes by Senate Democrats made during the Senate debate on whether to authorize Desert Storm, try to remember (1) that it was Iraq that invaded Kuwait without provocation, and (2) that the UN Security Council, yes even the UN, already voted to authorize the use of force if Iraq didn't withdraw from Kuwait.

~ `The president is wrong to have threatened Iraq with war.'

~ `President Bush appears to be on the verge of making a terrible mistake that will have tragic consequences for the whole world.'

~ `The administration is making a great mistake.'

~ `War would be a tragic mistake.'

~ `We are on a disastrous course.'

~ `The rush to combat now . . . is . . . tragically shortsighted.'

~ `The president . . . has moved in the wrong direction.'

~ `We are going to make such a tremendous blunder.'

~ `The president is marching this country toward a senseless and unnecessary war.'

~ *'The president should retreat* 'back to the defensive positions of the period up to Nov. 8th.'[67]

Less than two months after those defeatist comments by Democrat US Senators, in March of 1991:

~ Iraq forces were gone from Kuwait,

~ Iraq accepted a ceasefire and the American Troops were on their way home, and

~ George Herbert Walker Bush's poll ratings were at 89%.

As a result of Desert Storm, the Democrats had done nothing to change America's view as to which Party believed in America and its purpose and which Party should be trusted with the national defense. Despite such success, however, re-election would elude Bush 41 and the Republicans would not yet recapture Congress.

A Glaring Lesson In Political Economics for Republicans

If Republicans had burnished their credentials on national defense during Bush 41 with some enormous successes, then what could explain Bush's loss to Clinton in the 1992 Presidential Election? After all, there was no reversal on the issue of traditions and values. Those values were still under attack by the Left. From the continuing

---

[67] http://thomas.loc.gov/cgi-bin/query/z?r102:S13MR1-328:

efforts to remove God from the Public Square to whether the Pledge of Allegiance could be said in the classroom, or and whether school prayer would be allowed were still issues of the day that motivated Middle America. Beyond that, TV violence was of such concern that Congress passed legislation on the issue in 1990. The battles between pro-life forces and the abortion-on-demand crowd were, if anything, heating up *with the Left running to excess.* They were highlighted when women's groups faulted Madonna for making a record that featured an unmarried young woman choosing not to end her pregnancy.[68] Such is the definition of going too far.

In those ways and more, the Democrats were still antagonistic to traditional values and Middle America took affront and the Religious Right continued to flex its political muscle in response.

Thus, it is correct to say that on the issues of traditions and values and who better to defend America, nothing appreciable had changed – the Republicans were ahead on both issues.

What changed was George Herbert Walker Bush's mind on taxes. For many American voters that was unforgivable

---

[68] In the song *Papa Don't Preach* and accompanying video, a young woman decides to keep her child. Madonna was faulted for not expressing the alternative in the song – a clear indication of the Left's rising extremism on social issues which would be so prevalent in the 1990s.

and *it serves as a critical if not defining lesson for Republicans on how to stay ahead.*

~ ~ ~

I can recall driving down a windy road en route to meet a client the night of Bush's acceptance speech at the Republican convention. It seems odd to me now that I could have missed watching that speech on TV but the radio experience provided its own rewards. For many Republicans and the Nation, there was an uneasy sense about the resolve of Bush 41. It was an uneasiness well taken given that he had branded Reagan's pro-growth policies as "voodoo economics" eight years before.

By most accounts, it was one of Bush 41's best speeches. The highlight of that speech, which came through that night for radio and television audiences alike, was a set of lines that would define his Presidency rather than his significant achievements in foreign affairs:

"I'm the one who will not raise taxes.

"My opponent, my opponent now says, my opponent now says, he'll raise them as a last resort, or a third resort.

"But when a politician talks like that, you know that's one resort he'll be checking into.

"My opponent won't rule out raising taxes. But I will.

"And the Congress will push me to raise taxes, and I'll say no, and they'll push, and I'll say no, and they'll push again, and I'll say, to them,

""Read my lips: no new taxes."

There was no more memorable set of lines for Bush 41 that night or any other night. Even so, it was not the first time that Bush 41 had made the statement. The Republicans saw the effect the tax issue had during the Reagan-Mondale campaign. Mondale had made it clear that he would raise taxes and was crushed in the general election.

In an attempt to make that lesson orthodoxy for Republicans, in 1986, Grover Norquist, of the Americans for Tax Reform began promoting his "taxpayer protection pledge," which asked candidates to promise not to raise marginal tax rates on income. During the 1988 Presidential primaries, "George Bush pulled ahead of Bob Dole . . . by taking the pledge and bashing Dole for refraining."[69]

Those lessons were not lost on Bush's speech writer Peggy Noonan who wanted to emphasize the pledge for political effect. Jack Kemp, a co-author of Reagan's tax cuts and perhaps "the" political/economic conscience within

---

[69] **Our Enemy, The States,** *The federal Republicans are okay, but the governors need to get with it,* RAMESH PONNURU, http://www.nationalreview.com/nrd/trial/p.php?i=20050411&v=t&a=636

the Republican Party at the time, advocated Bush's pledge because it was economically right.

Just over two years later, Bush 41 changed his mind and the course of national politics.

At issue was a rising deficit brought on by excessive spending. The Democrats wanted a budget deal and the President wanted action. As an inducement to get President Bush to make a deal, the Democrats in Congress promised to trade spending cuts for new taxes. In making that offer, the Democrats placed Bush in the same position as the Republican Hoover, the Democrat Roosevelt, the Republican Eisenhower, the Democrat Kennedy and the Republican Reagan. Should he raise tax rates or lower them to increase revenues?

On November 5, 1990, President Bush sided with government, Hoover, Roosevelt, and Eisenhower and became a manager of government instead of a guarantor of economic freedom. Bush made that deal and he signed a budget deal that included an increase in tax rates. It was touted as a deal that would reduce the Budget deficit by $500 billion. The consequences would be real - but not as Bush intended.

Politically, it reignited the debate as to whether Bush 41 was a man of conviction and whether he was a true believer on the issue of pro-growth policies. Pat Buchanan made great hay of the flip flop in the lead up to his success in the

New Hampshire primary and Clinton would do the same in the general election.

Economically, the budget/tax bill was more of a flop than Bush's flip on taxes:

~ Just over a year later, in December of 1991 unemployment reached 7.1% as an outgrowth of a recession that began in 1990 – a recession exacerbated by Bush's tax increase,[70] and

~ The budget deficit for the year Bush signed the bill was $261.9 billion in Fiscal Year 1990 – *the lowest of his Presidency*. Two years later, Bush ran the *highest* deficit of his Presidency: $318.5 billion in FY1992.

The Bush experience on raising tax rates should be a clear political and economic lesson to all Republicans – no less a lesson than the Party should have learned under Eisenhower and Hoover. First, Bush failed to heed Reagan's 1982 admonition that "We don't have a trillion-dollar debt because we haven't taxed enough; we have a trillion-dollar debt because we spend too much." As if to confirm Reagan's warning, the Democrats never made good on their spending cuts pledge to Bush.

More importantly, however, was this economic fact: **In the face of difficult economic times, raising tax rates does**

---

[70] Remember, as Dr. Laffer would tell you, tax policy has more than an arithmetic effect on the economy. Tax cuts have a psychologically beneficial impact which spurs people to greater achievement. Tax hikes, quite understandably, have the opposite effect.

not result in higher tax revenues than otherwise would have been collected without the rate increase. Instead, as Larry Kudlow – a *New Conservative* - is fond of saying, it acts like a "wet blanket" and retards revenue growth over the long term. Ask Herbert Hoover who, obsessed with the deficit, raised the marginal income tax rate from 25% to 63% - a major contributing factor to the Great Depression.

Republican Governor Pete Wilson of California learned the same lesson at the same time. In 1991, Wilson increased taxes in response to a budget deficit. Years two and three of that rate increase actually resulted "in a revenue drop of $2 billion."[71] In total, it was a failed policy that played a considerable role in Republicans' poor showings in California for years to come.

So it is little wonder why the Bush budget deficit *increased* after the tax rate increases - as opposed to decreasing. In more glib than economic terms, long ago Winston Churchill capsulated the lesson which Republicans should have known by the early 1990s when he said:

---

[71] California's Tax Follies, States can't tax their way back to prosperity, By Lawrence J. McQuillan and Andrew M. Gloger, published in National Review Online, http://www.nationalreview.com/nrof_comment/comment-mcquillan040703.asp

"We contend that for a nation to try to tax itself into prosperity is like a man standing in a bucket and trying to lift himself up by the handle."

As 1992 wore on and Bush 41 looked at his watch,[72] it became entirely clear that he had no intention of jump-starting the economy by cutting taxes. The words and action of Kennedy and Reagan had no effect on President Bush. Rather than being bold like them, Bush acted like the Cautious Eisenhower who spoke of affordable tax cuts in the midst of a recession.

Although Bush was seemingly unmoved, the strategic effect on the Republican Party was real. By changing his mind, by abandoning pro-growth policies - Bush 41 blurred the lines between Republicans and Democrats. Republican economic policies were, once again, just like the policies of the Democrats.

Bush's failure to heed Reagan's and Kennedy's advice – the choice to abandon tax cuts, a critical Pillar of *The New Conservative Paradigm*, was the single largest reason

---

[72] President Bush, in a debate with Clinton, famously looked at his watch and was chastised by the press for being disconnected and aloof.

President Bush lost that fall to Bill Clinton – a candidate who campaigned by promising *a tax cut*.[73]

The careful observer will note that the presence of Ross Perot in the race was a major factor in Bush's loss as well. Perot garnered 19% of the vote - the majority of which votes many analysts believe would have gone to President Bush who lost to Clinton 43% to 38%.[74]

However, Perot was not much more than a single issue champion of deficit reduction brought on by out-of-control Washington spending. As such, the Perot factor was a symptom of the Bush's problem - not its cause. Further, Bush obviously did not learn the Reagan lesson on the philosophical importance of tax cuts. He abandoned the individual and the family and sided with the need to feed government. That played no small role in his loss.

Moreover, if Bush had not raised taxes but instead cut them, and had he insisted on reduction in spending – in short, had Bush led - the deficit would not have grown and probably would have diminished. So, in a very real way, Bush's failures made Perot relevant. Further, recall that

---

[73] Clinton's tax cut was designed for the "Middle Class" as opposed to a true pro-growth cut. Nevertheless, in the face of Bush's tax increase, the Republicans were without Reagan's signature economic argument.

[74] Special Prosecutor Lawrence Walsh's decision to indict Casper Weinberger just days before the election also played a role and, according to some, stalled a late comeback by President Bush.

Bush had a 89% approval rating 18 months before the election. As liberal pundit Mark Shields said, he was "a colossus astride the political landscape." So much so that prominent Democrats declined to enter the Democrat primaries assuming Bush wasn't beatable. But as history witnessed, rather than unshackle the American Spirit, Bush placated government. In doing so, he became beatable and he gave his enemies the weapons with which to defeat him – tax increases.

The moral of Bush's story therefore, was that Bush 41's weakness and abandoned promise gave rise to Perot and Clinton's victory, not the other way around. The enduring question of Republican politics everywhere is whether they will do the same again; whether they will follow Kennedy and Reagan to victory or Bush 41 (and Hoover) to defeat. *It need not be much more complicated than that.*

Clinton Bails out the Republican Party

If Bush 41 stumbled over tax cuts, the new fault line of national politics, Bill Clinton came to the rescue of Republicans. His assists to Republicans in taking back Congress were numerous and varied. Before we get to that important moment in history, it is worthy to note that there were certainly more prominent national Democrats available to run for President in late 1991 early 1992. The Democrats boasted such Presidential campaign veterans as Richard Gephardt, Joe Biden, Al Gore, and even the venerable Ted Kennedy. All deferred to lesser-knowns, however, because of Bush 41's 1991 high approval ratings in the afterglow of the first Iraq War. Those lesser-knowns included Paul Tsongas and a little known Governor from Arkansas, Bill Clinton. Despite a much talked about victory in New Hampshire, Paul Tsongas was not able to hold off the "Comeback Kid" Bill Clinton who we all know went on to become the Democrats' nominee.

In many ways, Clinton was the opposite of his general election opponent Bush 41. Clinton was young, energetic and telegenic. As it turned out, he also campaigned somewhat the opposite of the Democrat nominees that had gone before him. Clinton made that clear when he snubbed his party elders in a revealing speech to the Wharton School of Business at the University of Pennsylvania Philadelphia on April 16, 1992.

What was revealing was that Clinton had no intention of making the same mistakes as Mondale and Dukakis before him. Both had gone down in resounding defeats. For Clinton, there had to be another way, a New Democrat Way.

According to Clinton:

"If the Republicans' failed experiment in supply-side economics didn't produce growth, create upward mobility, or prepare millions of Americans to compete and win in the world economy, neither will the old Democratic theory that says we can just tax and spend our way out of any problem we face."

Beyond the rhetoric of false accusations against President Reagan,[75] Clinton clearly spoke against the orthodoxy of his Party by quoting the oft used Republican term about Democrats, i.e. that they "tax and spend."[76] Beyond speaking about it, Clinton became the first major Democrat nominee for President since Kennedy to make tax cuts a centerpiece of his candidacy. As of the 1992 General election, it would appear that Clinton understood Kennedy's and Reagan's lesson - *sort of.*

Rather than supply side cuts, Clinton's tax relief took the form of "targeted" tax cuts and included:

~ An investment tax credit and a new enterprise tax cut which Clinton claimed were "better than a capital gains tax cut because they reward investment in jobs, goods, and services,"

~ Making the research and development tax credit permanent,

~ A "Middle Class" tax cut.

---

[75] Reagan's supply-side growth produced 92 straight months of economic growth.

[76] By speaking critically of the Republicans and the Democrats, Clinton was striking the early chords of his method of leadership: triangulation.

History knows what became of those campaign promises but as a campaign tool it was a remarkable reversal. The Democrat Clinton campaigned for tax cuts (on behalf of Americans) while the Republican Bush had to answer for his tax increases (on behalf of the Government).

Less than a year after taking office, however, Bill Clinton abandoned his tax cut pledges and signed the largest tax increase in US History. Although the Major Media did not make Clinton pay for that flip-flop in the same way it did Bush 41, the Democrats in Congress certainly suffered in the very next election.

1994, The Democrats' Waterloo

Despite his claims to be a New Democrat, time would tell that Bill Clinton was indeed an old "tax and spend" Democrat.

Initially, there were hints that Clinton would be a New Democrat. After all, it was certainly true that in March of 1993, Clinton had his Vice-President Al Gore head up an initiative entitled the National Performance Review which was not totally unlike Reagan's Grace Commission. Gore's charter was to "reinvent" and streamline government. It was also true that Clinton sided against the American unions on December 8, 1993 by signing the North American Free Trade Agreement and thereby creating the largest free trade zone in the world. Thus, it could be argued that Clinton initially gave hints he intended to be a reformer.

But Clinton oversaw the adding of approximately 200,0000 pages to the Code of Federal Regulations during his first three years in office (and nearly 30,000 in the last 90 days of his Presidency) – nearly reversing the efforts of Reagan and matching the negative efforts of Carter. That old line act, however, was dwarfed by the Clinton's act of raising taxes.

At the time Clinton proposed his tax increase, the Democrats held a lead of 258 seats to 176 seats in the House of Representatives. In the Senate, the Democrats held a 57 – 43 seat advantage. Perhaps learning from the mistake of Bush 41, remarkably and tellingly, not a single Republican in either chamber of Congress voted for the Clinton tax increase.[77]

The combination of the Republicans' opposition to the Clinton defense cuts, along with Clinton's big government health care initiative and Clinton's promotion of less than traditional values and the emerging Clinton scandals,[78] meant that in 1994 the political parties were back to the same positions they had been at the end of Reagan's term.

---

[77] Grover Norquist deserves considerable credit as well for his No New Tax Pledge efforts.

[78] Clinton's first headline-grabbing act related to gays in the military.

The Republicans once again stood for the New Conservative Paradigm:

~ Pro- Growth policies including cutting taxes
~ Strong defense, and
~ Traditional ideals and values

The Democrats, on the other hand, once again stood for:

~ Raising taxes
~ A weaker defense, and
~ Attacking America's traditional values

To reinforce those differences, and in an effort to stand *for something*, not simply *against the incumbent party*, the Republican brain trust in the House (including Newt Gingrich, Dick Armey among others) along with the help of Republican pollster Frank Luntz, another ***New Conservative***, in a fit of strategic brilliance, championed the Contract with America. The Contract with America contained a variety of tax cuts, including capital gains cuts and indexation, a $500 per child tax credit, and marriage tax penalty relief.

On the traditions and values front, among other items, it sought (a) to discourage illegitimacy and teen pregnancy by prohibiting welfare to mothers under 18 years of age, and (b) to deny increased AFDC for additional children while on welfare, and (c) to enact what would be called "two-years-and-out provisions" which required work in exchange for benefits.

All in all, the Contract with America was a marvelous political marketing tool which clearly delineated the difference between the parties and gave voters a compelling reason to vote the majority Democrats out of power. It also marked the first time in American History that a Party's Congressional candidates ran on a unified platform. The results of election night November 8, 1994 would indeed be the Democrats' Waterloo. The Republicans gained control of both chambers of Congress, the House and the Senate for the first time in forty years – since Eisenhower championed affordable tax cuts and, in doing so, turned Republicans out into the political wilderness.

In short, the Republicans were now ahead on the three pillars of ***The New Conservative Paradigm***. More significantly, the Republican Party had completed its comeback from its depths – when the Democrats were identified 1) as the party of tax cuts, 2) as strong on defense, and 3) as the safeguard of families. Statistically, the reversal and its effects are difficult to challenge.

The House of Representatives and the Senate from 1953 to 2005

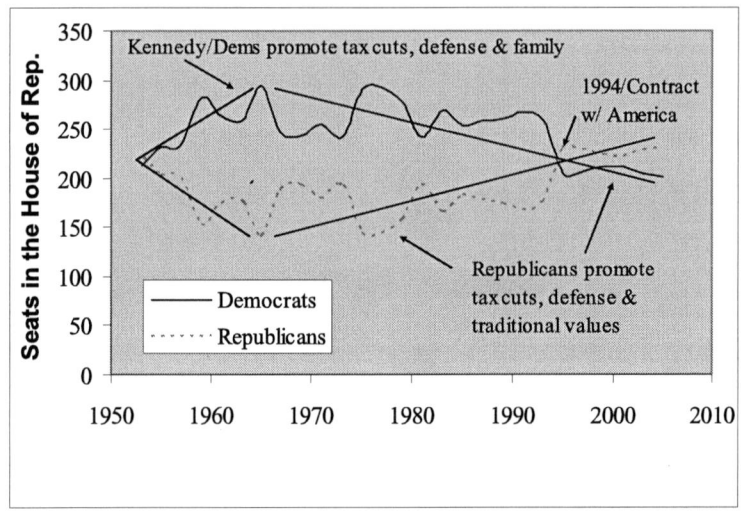

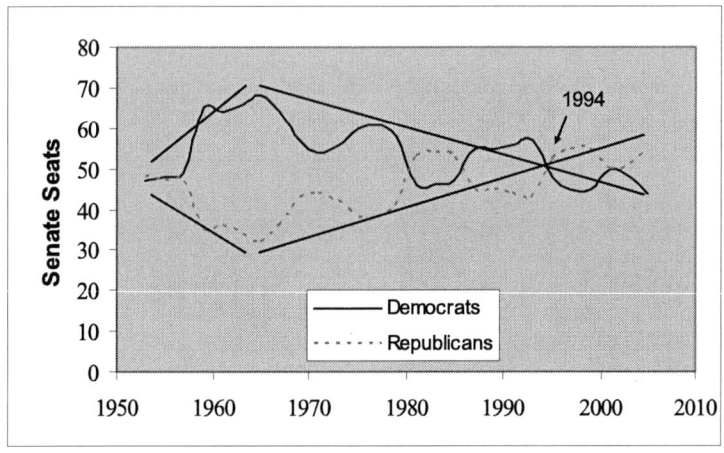

Our story was not ending, however. Indeed, the balance of the Clinton Presidency and the start of Bush 43 would only serve to solidify the *New Conservative Paradigm.*

STRENGTHENING THE PARADIGM

1994 TO 2004

As we have seen, the Congressional Elections of 1994 were the culmination of a political reversal first begun under Ronald Reagan. Republicans took pride in *their new-found status and knew it could not have happened without Reagan's leadership. The Democrat leadership, on* the other hand, had trouble accepting that there was a reversal and few understood it then (or even now) that it happened with their help. In fact, in the 12 years between 1994 and 2006, the leaders of the Democrat Party, with few notable exceptions, were in denial as to the cause of their fate - criticizing Republicans leaders as not smart[79] and voters as ill-informed – rather than truly assessing their own actions.

It would not seem to be a difficult task for a political party, in the position the Democrats were in the late 1990s, to look back to the last time they had an overwhelming majority in Congress, 1965 – and then assess the positions they held at the time and reinvigorate their party by reviving those policies. The story of the remainder of the Clinton Presidency, and Bush 43's first term, however, was not that story. To the contrary, the beliefs of each Party in their positions on the pillars of *The New Conservative Paradigm* appear to have deepened - and with them – so too the Republican majority in Congress.

---

[79] The Democrat National Committee Chairman Howard Dean has taken such rhetoric to a new level by describing Republicans and/or their leaders as "brain dead," "evil," "corrupt" and "liars."

In looking at these charts, covering the last three Presidential elections, or from the time Clinton was elected to Bush 43's re-election, note both the trend line and the increase since 2000 in what was the Republican majority until 2006 in Congress.

The US House of Representatives

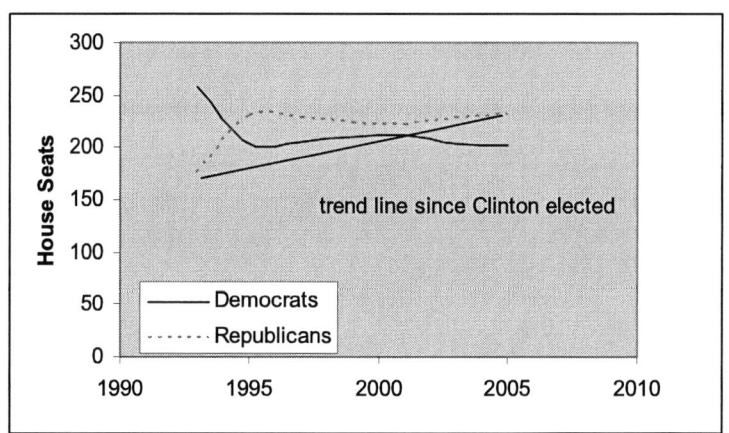

The US Senate

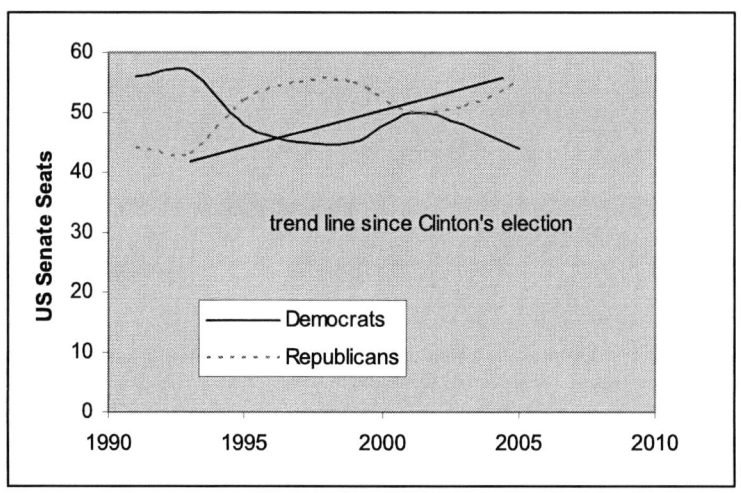

Why The New Conservative Paradigm Deepened
Pillar Number One: The Tax Side of Pro-Growth Policies

Why did the Paradigm deepen? For starters, under President Clinton "individual income taxes (excluding Social Security) . . . climbed from 7.8% of GDP to more than 10%. That marked **the highest rate in U.S. history**."[80] How dramatic a rise was that? "Following the Reagan tax cuts of the early 1980s, federal income taxes paid by individuals in fiscal 1984 fell to 7.8% of GDP and then stayed within a relatively narrow range of approximately 7.6% to 8.5% of GDP until the 1993 [Clinton] tax hike."[81] So much for freedom and property rights – Clinton, in dramatic fashion, sided with government over the individual.

As you consider that dramatic increase in taxes since 1993, remember:

~ No Republican in Congress voted for the 1993 Clinton tax increase – or any income tax increase since; and

~ "In September 1999, President Clinton vetoed a $792 billion tax cut over 10 years that the Republican Congress

---

[80] Clinton's Untenable Taxation I, The serious economic problem of the 1993 tax increase, William P. Kucewicz,
http://www.nationalreview.com/nrof_kucewicz/kucewicz103001.shtml

[81] Id.

sent to him as a pre-election year ploy. Al Gore, the Democrats' nominee-in-waiting, previewed his 2000 campaign language by denouncing the GOP gambit as a "risky scheme."[82]

~ Those high tax rates were responsible for the recession that got under way during Clinton's last year and spilled over into Bush's first term.[83]

In contrast to Clinton tax increases, President George W. Bush passed four tax cuts in his first term. On its face, that alone cemented the Republicans lead in **Pillar Number One**, *Pro Growth tax cuts. But something more, just under the surface had occurred – and it presents a strong lesson for Republicans today.*

The first Bush tax cut was signed on June 7, 2001. According to PBS:

---

[82] http://www.americanpresident.org/history/bushgeorgew/biography/domesticaffairs.common.shtml

[83] The Clinton recession began in the 3rd quarter of 2000 – a predictable result given the highest tax burden in US history. It is also important to note that recession started before President Bush was elected. See the "Last Economic Recession Began Under Clinton, Despite Rewrites By The Left," by Don Luskin (May 17, 2004).
http://www.capmag.com/article.asp?ID=3691.

"While the bill got significant Democratic support, *most Democrat leaders criticized it as far too large to meet other national priorities*, such as increased spending on education and a Medicare prescription drug benefit, and said it would *cost* at least $4 trillion in the second decade."[84]

Bush's second tax cut came in 2002 and met with similar disdain from Democrats. Hillary Clinton questioned whether the 2002 tax cut was appropriate when, in response to Bush 43's 2002 State of the Union address, she stated: "We'll have a better idea of the ramifications of what we've heard tonight, when we *match it to the budget*."

Not to be outdone, Democrat Senate Leader Tom Daschle stated:

"We can't go back to deficit spending. *The tax cut must be affordable* and responsible."

Howard Dean, Democrat Presidential aspirant, captured their spirit in full, however, when he said during a 2003 primary debate:

"We cannot afford all of the tax cuts, [all the programs we want], and balancing the budget. Let's call this one right. Let's be fiscally responsible and balance the budget."

---

[84] http://www.pbs.org/newshour/updates/june01/tax_6-7.html . Democratic Senate Leader Tom Daschle was among those with "fiscal" objections. See "Demagoguing the President's Tax Cuts" Joseph Perkins, http://www.signonsandiego.com/news/op-ed/perkins/20020111-9999_1e11perkins.html

In April of 2005, Hillary chimed in once again and said: "[W]e're getting tax cuts that we don't need and *America cannot afford*."

After reading those quotes, ask yourself who those Democrats sound more like?

Eisenhower of the three recessions:

"We cannot *afford* to reduce taxes, reduce income until we have in sight a program of expenditure that shows that the factors of income and outgo will be balanced."

Kennedy: of the three years of soaring revenues:

"I repeat: our practical choice is not between a tax-cut deficit and budgetary surplus. It is between two kinds of deficits: a chronic deficit of inertia, as the unwanted result of inadequate revenues and a restricted economy; or a temporary deficit of transition, resulting from a *tax cut designed to boost the economy, increase tax revenues*, and achieve--and I believe this can be done--a budget surplus."

In truth, it is inescapable but to conclude that the Democrat leaders adopted, wholesale, Eisenhower's notion that tax cuts must be *affordable* – the mantra of a minority party that produced 40 years of Republican wilderness in the Congress. To press the point, even Al Gore, who called the Bush tax cuts a "risky scheme" appeared to be channeling Barry Goldwater's 1964 criticism of the Kennedy tax cuts as "gimmickry."

It is also fair to say that the Democrats and Republicans truly had reversed positions from the time of Kennedy and Goldwater to Clinton and Bush. The Democrats during the Clinton years sided with Government and the Republicans sided with individuals and families. As a result, by the first term of George W. Bush the Parties' respective positions were solidified on the first Pillar of *The New Conservative Paradigm*, pro-freedom *tax cuts* – the new fault line of American politics.

It should be no wonder then, how the Republicans increased their majority in the Congress during that period of time.[85]

Pillar Number One: Reform Side of Pro-Growth Policies

It was Bill Clinton who announced that the era of Big Government was over. Unfortunately, neither he nor Bush

---

[85] Thoughtful observers will point out that despite his tax increases Clinton was re-elected. While that is true, the problem with that observation is that the Republicans nominated Senator Bob Dole as their candidate in 1996. During his decades of service, Sen. Dole was against the Kennedy tax cuts and, as a Republican leader, shepherded through tax increases in the Senate. Simply stated, Dole was not a convincing voice for tax cuts. Even though Dole eventually came out for a tax cut, he previously refused to take the "No New Tax Pledge" and was battered by Pat Buchanan in the Republican primary for that refusal. When he did come out for a tax cut, it was a belated effort and made in earnest only after Clinton had "defined" Dole through early and relentless advertising. As a result, there simply was not any convincing definition between the candidates as there could have been – even after the nomination of Jack Kemp for Vice President.

43 ended the era of spending increases.[86] Bush, however, sought to pick up the mantle of reform last brandished by President Reagan. At the outset of his first term, Bush 43 was able to pass an Education Reform Bill which sought accountability from our education establishment. His next achievement was a Tax Reform Bill that was eventually accelerated and produced a recovery out of the ashes of 9/11 and the Clinton recession. Bush then pushed for complete tax reform by naming a tax reform panel headed by former Senator Connie Mack and signed into law bankruptcy reform.

Bush continued his Reform efforts by pushing for government management initiatives such as competitive sourcing. He also sought reform in the manner in which the Government cares for people in the form of his Faith Based Initiative – a reform that strengthened his commitment to **Pillar Number Three**. Bush also sought or achieved degrees of bankruptcy reform, legal reform, medical liability reform and the mother of all domestic reforms – Social Security.

---

[86] FY 1993 spending under Clinton was $1.4 trillion, $1.46 trillion in '94, $1.51 trillion in '95, $1.56 trillion in '96, $1.6 trillion in '97, $1.65 in '98, $1.7 trillion in '99, $1.8 trillion in '00. Under Bush 41, the increases accelerated to $1.86 trillion in '01, $2.0 trillion in '02, $2.16 trillion in '03, $2.3 trillion in '04, $2.48 trillion in '05, $2.6 trillion in '06 and $2.9 trillion in '07.

Beyond those reforms, in what appeared at the time as a stroke of genius at the outset of his second term, Bush was able to cast his foreign policy in Reform terms. No longer a policy just to root out al Qaeda, Bush's policy became a policy to Reform oppressive governments and spread democracy throughout the world. Thusly, Bush cast his Presidency as a Reformist Presidency domestically and internationally.

The Republican message of reform, however, was not limited to President Bush. In California, in the wake of the failed policies of the legislature and Governor Davis – policies which brought the state to the brink of bankruptcy – Californians reformed the State by recalling the Democrat Governor and replacing him with a Republican Governor who promised to take reform to a new level by "blowing-up" the old boxes of the government apparatus. Thereafter, Governor Schwarzenegger made Reform his priority by passing budget reforms, workers' compensation reform, and regulatory reforms. In 2005, he made redistricting reform, pension reform and education reform national topics.

The response by the Democrat leadership to all of those Reforms was and is a predictable *NO*. In 2005, despite the passage of months, the national Democrats refused to provide a single constructive alternative reform to President Bush's Social Security Reform initiative other than raising taxes. In California, the leadership of the Democrat Party responded with even less – they offered no meaningful reforms.[87]

As 2005 drew to a close, it was more than evident that the Republican Party was able to cast itself as the Reform Party and the Democrats the defenders of Big Government – a moniker that is perhaps worse than the *Party of No* and clearly out of step with the times. It is also ironic given that the Democrats have adopted the use of the word "progressive" to describe their Party. Simply stated, a Party cannot be for progress when in practice it does no more than defend existing – failing – government programs.

Pillar Number Two: Protectors of the Homeland

If we start with the proposition that Americans, in 1992, trusted the Republican Party more than the Democrats on the issue of which Party believed in America's purpose and protecting our homeland, then the events of the remainder of the 1990s did little to change that view.

Indeed, when considering the defense of America, from the outset of the Clinton administration, it was apparent to many that Clinton and the Democrats were "raiding the

---

[87] Facing rigorous opposition to those reforms and a $100 million smear campaign against Arnold Schwarzenegger, those 2005 reforms did not pass. However, Arnold Schwarzenegger won a resounding reelection victory in 2006, by promising to hold the line on new taxes against an old-line Democrat, Phil Angelides, who promised to raise taxes.

defense budget to fund new social spending."[88] According to a Republican backbencher, Congressman Joel Healy of Colorado, not the most partisan of the bunch:

"Under the Clinton defense blueprint, by 1999 the defense budget will account for only 2.8 percent of gross domestic product. At no time since before World War II have we dropped below 4.4 percent of gross domestic product . . .

During the same time, domestic spending is slated to increase by 12 percent, entitlements by 38 percent. What effect does this have on our military? Although only ten percent of the Clinton defense cuts have been made, enlistment in the Armed Forces is down. The quality of recruits is dropping. The voluntary military concept which has worked so well in this country is threatened."[89]

A year later, the liberal press in the form of the New York Times upped the ante by stating that: "production of new tanks, planes, and ships can be put off for a decade or more" in support of their claim that the Clinton defense cuts did not go far enough. The Washington Post joined in by claiming the cuts represented "incrementalism."[90]

In actual numbers, Clinton defense budgets did indeed provide real cuts to our military budget. To be fair, Bush 41

---

[88] Floor speech of Joel Healy, July 19, 1994, http://thomas.loc.gov/cgi-bin/query/z?r103:H19JY4-7:

[89] Id.

[90] The Destruction of National Defense, John T. Correlly, http://www.afa.org/magazine/1993/05edit93.asp

started the reductions as part of the "peace dividend" from the end of the Cold War. The problem for the Democrats, however, was that Clinton, whose Presidency had no strong foreign policy successes that could compete with the successes of Bush 41 or Reagan, *noticeably increased* the reduction from those offered by Bush 41.

As such, since the Democrats were behind on the issue to begin with – and by a significant margin - the additional cuts only served to reinforce the existing view of the Democrats. Additional reinforcement occurred when the savings that were anticipated from the dividend were spent on domestic programs - making Clinton a *tax and spend* Democrat in the grand tradition of his Party.

Far worse than those cuts, however, was the fact that the Clinton policies, over time, proved to be weak and, as seminal author Richard Miniter wrote, "unleashed global terror."[91]

Clinton's False Sense of Security

For those not paying close attention to the Clinton era defense policies, frankly, his policies did not appear clearly damaging to the United States. Clinton's assist in Northern Ireland resulted in an opening to the long standing divisions

---

[91] Losing bin Laden, How bill Clinton's failures Unleashed Global Terror, Richard Miniter

in the area. Clinton's bombing of Bosnia appeared to end a conflict via an air war. Clinton "showed" that America was interested in Middle East peace by attempting to broker a grand deal to which Yasser Arafat simply would not take yes for an answer. Thus, many a casual observer claimed that the US was at peace.

Many less than casual observers on the Left also came to that erroneous conclusion - if not peddled that false sense of security. Chief among them was Hillary Clinton who claimed that Bill Clinton "gave us eight years of peace" during her 2004 Democrat Convention Speech delivered to like-minded delegates. Time, however, has made it quite clear that that was not the case.

Glimpses that turned to glare of Clinton's weak foreign policy surfaced during his Presidency in the form of:

~ Clinton's failure to respond with much more than a police investigation to the 1993 al Qaeda bombings of the Twin Towers – eight years before they were brought down within months of the end of Clinton's Presidency – the planning of which occurred largely during Clinton's Presidency.

~ Clinton "destruction of an empty building in central Baghdad" in response to Saddam Hussein's assassination plot against Bush 41.[92]

---

[92] Id. at 55.

~ Clinton's failure to truly hold Hussein accountable – with other than bombing raids - despite countless UN resolutions and his countless violations.

Perhaps, at least in retrospect, the worst action taken by Clinton was the ignominious withdrawal of American troops from Somalia after the downing of a Blackhawk helicopter. That battle became a Hollywood movie and more importantly, the withdrawal engendered the following response from Osama bin Laden:

"Our boys went to Somalia and prepared themselves carefully for a long war . . . Our boys were shocked by the low morale of the American soldier, and they realized that the American soldier was just a paper tiger. He was unable to endure the strikes that were dealt to his army, so he fled, and America had to stop all its bragging."

After reading that, can there be any doubt whatsoever that bin Laden believed that leadership under Bill Clinton was not the same leadership that induced Iran to release the American hostages on the eve of the Reagan Presidency? Can there be any doubt that the meager responses by the Clinton administration to the first al Qaeda attack on the Twin Towers - and the seven others during the Clinton years against U.S. interests – convinced bin Laden that he could plan and get away with flying planes into the Twin

Towers?[93] Only the most ardent partisan could think otherwise and, in time, most of Americans would as well.

As a result, America closed the Clinton years with a clear understanding that the Republicans maintained a clear edge on **Pillar Number Two, Belief in America and its defens**e.

The early success of George W. Bush in continuing to reinforce Americans' view of which Party was ahead on the Second Pillar can be summed up in two words: "Security Moms." The designation was part of the never-ending desire on the part of the Media and consultants to market the latest "swing" voter group which the national parties were required to court. If you recall, the 1990s saw the rise of the "Soccer Moms." For them, the Parties were told that they had to address their concerns on such "kitchen table" issues as education and child care. As the first post-9/11 Presidential election in 2004 drew near, however, the "Soccer Mom" designation gave way to "Security Moms."

The Bush Administration's response to 9/11 was nothing if not comprehensive. It included a war in Afghanistan to replace an ugly, brutal regime that harbored, if not

---

[93] The al Qaeda attacks/plots included: (1) the December 1992 Aden Hotel attacks in Yemen, (2) 1993 car bomb attack on New York's Twin Towers, (3) 1993 attacks in Somalia including the downing of a Blackhawk helicopter, (4) 1995 al Qaeda plan to bomb multiple US planes code named "Project Bojinka" discovered, (5) al Qaeda bombs US interests in Riyadh, Saudi Arabia, (6) 1998 near simultaneous bombings by al Qaeda of US embassies in Nairobi & Dar es Salaam killing 200 injuring 4500, (7) 2000 failed attack on the USS Sullivans in Yemen discovered.

sponsored, Osama bin Laden and al Qaeda. It included the Patriot Act and the Department of Homeland Security.[94] It has included countless efforts to win the War on Terror – efforts that were chronicled by Richard Miniter, a *New Conservative,* in his book **Shadow War, The Untold Story of How America is Winning the War on Terror** – his follow up best seller to his first best seller, **Losing bin Laden**. And, of course, it included removing Saddam Hussein from Iraq in contrast to Clinton's bombing of Iraq.

All the while, there can be little doubt that leading Democrats fought the Bush Administration efforts. Some blamed US policy for 9/11 in the latest manifestation of the "Blame America First" crowd. Others claimed that a war in Afghanistan was unwinnable and we would be bogged down in the mountain winters of that region. Before the Iraq War started, the Left claimed that the war would result in hundreds of thousands of deaths. After the war began, and despite US tanks rolling into Baghdad, the Left claimed that we were losing the war. As for Iraqi elections, they too were claimed not to be possible. Countless Democrats decried our break with France, Germany and Russia on the issue and,

---

[94] Democrats may rightly claim that President Bush resisted the Department of Homeland Security at first. Nevertheless, he came to champion it and will get the credit, or perhaps the blame, just as Clinton claims credit for welfare reform – which was a Republican/Contract with America idea.

perhaps in response, they ran a Presidential Candidate in 2004 – John Kerry - who was an "internationalist."

Few on the Left backtracked, however, even after revelations of the French and Russian Iraqi bribes (which explained their opposition to the wars). Nor did the incredible success of the Afghani and Iraqi elections have any effect. Instead, the Left could be seen pounding away at America and its purpose in the World - all the while ignoring the misdeeds of those fighting against the US. Although Americans' impatience with the war was beginning to show in 2005, the Democrats were reinforcing their weak security credentials leaving the Republicans firmly ahead on Pillar Number Two.

Pillar Number Three:
Respect for Traditions and Values

It would appear beyond the point of argument that the Clinton years reinforced the divide between the parties on the 3rd pillar of *The New Conservative Paradigm*, respect for traditions and values. Indeed, for most of the Nation, including many Democrats, the Clinton years were a bit too much for the senses.

Although Clinton enjoyed a certain status as a Southern Governor replete with Baptist ties - a factor that helped him in his election over the irreligious Dole - who can forget that

Clinton's first high profile act was an initiative seeking social change: Clinton's Gays in the Military program?[95] It was undertaken within days after his inauguration and did not get "resolved" until July of that year – and wound up satisfying very few when the "Don't Ask, Don't Tell Policy" was adopted. Thereafter, the nation was entreated to the sordid details of Jennifer Flowers, Paula Jones and, of course, Monica Lewinsky. Combined with Whitewater, the fundraising scandals and ultimately Impeachment, for many people in the Country, there was a perceived risk that turning on the television might not be in their child's best interest.

Beyond the Clinton chronicles, if the 1980s saw the zenith of the Christian Right's influence on Republican politics, the 1990s saw the rise of the far Left's influence on, if not control of, the Democrat Party. Their agenda seemed to accelerate during this tumultuous period.

The Drive to Remove God from the Public Square Continues.

There was no easing up on the drive by the Left to change traditions and values as they related to God in the

---

[95] Contrast that with Reagan's first high profile act which was the complete deregulation of oil and gas.

Public Square during this period. In the decade of the 1990s, examples abounded:

~ In 1993, long before the 2003 Alabama case, the "Ten Commandments, despite the fact that they . . . are depicted in engraved stone in the U.S. Supreme Court" were barred from the Georgia Court House.[96]

~ Also in 1993, historical classic artwork was barred from public schools because of its religious theme - this time in South Dakota.[97]

~ In 1994, it was ruled unconstitutional for a school graduation ceremony to contain an opening or closing prayer.[98]

After the century turned, a new height was reached in 2002. The liberal 9th Circuit Court of Appeals ruled that the Pledge of Allegiance was unconstitutional based on the inclusion of the phrase "Under God" – a ruling which, by its logic, necessarily would require the removal of the words "In God We Trust" from all of our currency. Even leaders of the

---

[96] *Harvey v. Cobb County* – an appeals case heard in Georgia and cited in David Barton's *Original Intent*, The Courts, The Constitution & Religion.

[97] *Washegesic v. Bloomingdale Public Schools*, 33 F.3d 679 (6th Cir. 1994) [held that the display of a portrait of Christ, a copy of Warren Sallman's "Head of Christ," in a hallway outside the gymnasium violated the Establishment Clause] cited in *Original Intent*.

[98] *Harris v. Joint School District No. 241*, 41F.3d 447 (9th Cir. 1994). Of course, every session of Congress begins with an invocation and as we have seen, the Congress requested that Washington institute a day of Prayer on the same day they approved of the final wording of the 1st Amendment.

Democrat party had to recoil given the implications – but few doubt those implications remain the intentions of the Left.

Alternative Lifestyles and Mainstream America

The Left's social agenda in the 1990s, however, was not limited to the removal of God from the Public Square. In ways too demonstrable and troubling for the majority of Americans, the advocacy of alternative lifestyle rights appeared to move toward center stage during that time. Keep in mind for purposes of this book and as we review this history, the point of the discussion is only to put the issue in historical context as it affects politics at large – not to decide the issue. In that light, for many Americans, the push on social issues by the Left and their Democrat patrons has been too much and too fast and that worked against the Democrats politically.

Keep in mind that the 1990s were certainly not the first time that gay issues were brought before Americans nor the first time the Country struggled to come to grips with related issues. By the 1990s, however, the role of political parties regarding gay rights was becoming more defined. Prior to that, the parties were not always far apart on the issue. During the 1950s, the US taxpayer paid for a government report that concluded that "homosexuals . . . are not proper persons to be employed in Government . . ."[99]

In the 1960s, Hollywood, not surprisingly, led in a different direction when it revised its production code to include the following language "homosexuality and other sexual aberrations may now be treated with care, discretion and restraint." In the 1970s, Hollywood productions began featuring gay life, a theme that seems to pervade many of the movies and television programs of today.

In a glimpse of things to come, the 1980 Democrat Convention featured an openly gay "candidate" for Vice President (Mel Boozer) who addressed the convention. In 1984, in where else but Berkeley, California became the first municipality to extend "spousal" benefits to domestic partners. In 1989, Congress only "censured" openly gay Mass. Representative Barney Frank despite his permitting a homosexual prostitute to use Frank's home for his activities. That same year, the American Bar Association, home to many a trial lawyer, overwhelmingly passed a resolution seeking federal legislation in favor of rights for gays and lesbians.

If the 1990s were not the first decade that the issue of gay rights arose, it certainly became the decade that the courts and the legislatures of America became the forum for

---

[99] Interim Report submitted to the Committee on Expenditures in the Executive Departments by its Subcommittee on Investigations pursuant to S. Res. 280 (81st Congress).

the gay rights issues. US restrictions on the immigration of gays were rescinded in 1990, California Governor Pete Wilson vetoed a gay employment rights bill in 1991, the Kentucky Supreme Court struck down a sodomy law in 1992 while in the same year Colorado voters banned state and municipal rights for gays – a vote that touched off similar drives throughout the country. In 1993, the Hawaii Supreme Court addressed the gay marriage issue in the same year the Massachusetts Senate became the first state to approve a law to protect gay students against discrimination in public schools.

Similar processes continued throughout the 1990s (and to this day) which included a loss by one vote of a federal law in 1996 that would have banned employment discrimination against gays and the eventual signing of the Marriage and Defense Act. The drive had quickened to the point that, in 1997, the National Gay and Lesbian Task Force was able to boast that "Gay rights legislation at the city and county level has advanced at a dramatic pace in the 1990s" which included gay rights ordinances in 157 US cities and counties at that time.

Today, the gay movement seeks, and in many cases has achieved, not just greater anti-discrimination laws but marriage/civil union rights, parenting rights and/or the re-defining of the family unit, health care rights and curriculum changes in schools reflective of their movements.

Again, the point of raising the issue, in this book, is not to debate the merits of gay rights, nor is it to determine who is right or wrong in God's eyes – it is not even to recommend a political resolution. Indeed, like the issue of abortion, it may well be that a "resolution" of the issue is elusive. The point of raising the issue is two-fold.

First, a considerable majority of Americans disagree with Far Left's social agenda and the pace of change they seek - a significant amount of which unwaveringly if not virulently so. Witness the rise in the number of States passing bans on same-sex marriage.[100] Of those not against the agenda, many are libertarian to the extent that they are willing to live and let live *provided* they are not required by government or anyone else to give up their own traditions and values.

Unlike the issue of abortion, however – and this is the crux of the matter for many - whereas someone's decision or agenda related to abortion *may* not directly affect their neighbor (your neighbor could have an abortion without your knowledge), in the view of many Americans, the Far Left's agenda *and tactics* with regard to gay rights necessarily does.

No greater example of that could be found than in the public school context where the gay agenda is pushed on children of remarkably young age. For the vast majority on the Right, that is not acceptable. For many in the middle, it is pushing too much on their children at an early age – and,

---

[100] For instance, in 2006, Tennessee voters passed a gay marriage ban 81% to 19%.

the irony is not lost on a majority that the Left simultaneously demands that the community stay out of their bedrooms at the same time they seek to push their agenda into school rooms.

Of course, the same analysis holds true for the God in the Public Square issue. For the Left, success is not defined by the tolerance they so eagerly demand of others - but, instead, by their ability to take away the traditions of others. Such hostile takeover attempts of any aspect of a culture are rarely greeted with indifference let alone an issue so central to the very meaning of life.

Thus, it is certainly no wonder that on all those issues the so-called Christian Right has fought back seeking to hold onto the traditions and values they know and cherish. In truth, however, this coalition of those willing to hold onto their traditions and values and ideals - if for no other reason than to have their children grow up like them - without all the background noise of the modern world – is much broader than the fit of any label such as "traditional values."

As for the second reason, the issue that is most relevant to *The New Conservative Paradigm*, simply stated, Americans realize that it is the leadership of the Democrats, often referred to as the San Francisco Democrats, that supports that agenda – an agenda which runs counter to the simple life so many have known and want for their children.

So, whether in the form of their preference for the nostalgia of Reagan's "Shining City on a Hill" or the decency of President George W. Bush, contrasted with the Clinton trysts, as of 2004, the majority of Americans believed that the Republican Party was ahead on the Third Pillar of ***The New Conservative Paradigm***, preserving our traditions and values. Given the hold the Far Left has on the Democrat party and their dedication to that agenda, it is a lead not likely to be lost for some time to come.

REPUBLICANS RETURN CLINTON'S FAVOR 2004 TO 2006

"Nothing is easier than the expenditure of public money.
It doesn't appear to belong to anyone.
The temptation is overwhelming to bestow it on somebody."
Republican, President Calvin Coolidge

As we have seen, leading up to the 1994 Congressional election, the Republicans' best friend was Bill Clinton. He started off his Presidency with a nod toward the Left by pushing a policy change for homosexuals serving in the military. Not long after, he broke his campaign promise of a tax cut and instead signed a massive tax increase. Republicans voted against the tax bill in unison and in doing so, gave greater meaning to the vision that Reagan laid out in the decade before. In a very real way, Clinton coalesced Republicans in a way that not even Reagan did.

Republicans followed up on their opposition to the Clinton tax hike with the *Contract With America*. It was the first time in Congressional history that candidates for the House of Representatives ran on a unified and specific platform. By giving the voters a clear choice, a choice that highlighted two of the three **Pillars of the New Conservative Paradigm** (Pro-Growth/Reform and Respect for Traditions and Values), Republicans took back the Congress.

Nine out of ten of the provisions of the *Contract With America* were then enacted – and - for sometime thereafter, Congressional Republicans acted liked reformists. In doing so, and by rejecting calls for further tax hikes, Congressional Republicans strengthened the Republicans' considerable lead on **Pillar Number One: Pro-growth policies and reform** and renewed their commitment to **Pillar Number Two: Respect for Tradition and Traditional Values.**

From 2004 to 2006, once again, *things had changed.* The 24-hour news cycle/Internet age had taken hold in earnest. In the competition for ratings, the Media and websites exaggerate events and those exaggerations, in turn, foster exaggerated responses from politicians – most often in the form of new government programs or spending to "solve" each and every perceived inequity. That dynamic is, of course, a dangerous and near irresistible invitation to become a proponent of government – and it is an especially bad temptation given that we are more than a quarter century since Reagan aptly stated, "The nine most terrifying words in the English language are 'I'm from the government and I'm here to help.'"

It is against that backdrop that we can view how, shortly after Bush's re-election in 2004, the Republican leaders began to return Clinton's favor. The obvious change between the Republican leaders from 1994 and the Republican leaders of the 2005/2006 Congress manifested itself for all to see in 2005. By many accounts, 2005 became the year of spending. The 2005 federal transportation bill was a monument to pork barrel spending. It featured a mega, mega-million-dollar-bridge, in Alaska, to serve a virtually uninhabited island – aptly referred to as the Bridge to Nowhere.

The Republican Leadership reached a rhetorical low in September of 2005. House Majority Leader, Republican Tom Delay, who helped Republicans and the reform movement in the 1990s, on that date, declared an "ongoing victory" against fat in the US budget. Incredibly, he claimed that there was no fat left to cut in the federal budget. He concluded his dispiriting thoughts by stating that "After 11 years of Republican majority we've pared [the budget] down pretty good." Conservatives everywhere, Independents in many places and even Democrats, could not take his comment seriously – although the transformation of Republican leadership would have serious effects.

Then, in response to Hurricane Katrina, in October of 2005, the Republican Congress passed an aid package that, in all likelihood, will end up larger, in gross dollars, than the entire 1970 federal budget - which was roughly $190 billion dollars.

Through it all, President Bush did not blemish his record of failing to impose a single veto. According to *New Conservative* Mona Charen, "The Republican Congress . . . increased spending by 33 percent since George W. Bush took office" and "Inflation-adjusted spending on the combined budgets of the 101 largest programs Republicans vowed to eliminate in 1995 has grown by 27 percent." After all was said and done, in October of 2005, Congressional approval ratings sank to depressing lows – reflecting the fact that there is no majority in this Country that approves of monumental spending.

In 2006, the Congressional Republicans did – well – nothing particularly good that was visible. Instead, they kept spending - for which there is no majority constituency. There also is no question that Hastert, Frist - and Bush by extension - wanted to do nothing more than run out the clock in '06. They were, in effect, looking over their shoulders instead of forging ahead. There was no evident vision and no plan – let alone good communication. But that was not for a lack of ideas or problems to fix. It was a lack of leadership.

Indeed, despite the impending expiration of the Bush tax cuts – and despite the fact that the Country has no appetite for tax increases – and despite the fact that tax cuts have been the one common winning issue for the last 7 Presidential contenders, the renewal of the tax cuts was barely mentioned let alone made a centerpiece of the 2006 election.

As for reform, that didn't happen either – and there were plenty of opportunities. Immigration? – the answer is fairly obvious. They discussed it and in the end came up with almost nothing. Social Security and Medicare? The answer is fairly obvious as well. They discussed it and in the end came up with exactly nothing.

All of this is to say that by November of 2006, the Republican leadership was offering voters little in the way of a vision for the future and certainly no identifiable plan. ***Instead of staying ahead, they allowed themselves to be caught.***

It certainly did not have to be so. After all, the Democrat leaders still did not offer much in the form of a positive agenda – no *Contract With America*, no 100 day plan, not much more than they had in previous years when they earned the moniker of the Party of *No*. Indeed, rather than offering a plan, their Party leaders seemed to go into hiding down the stretch: Pelosi, Reid, Murtha, Durbin, Dodd, Kennedy and the like were *Missing In Action*.

In politics, they say you can't beat something with nothing. That axiom applied well as to how the Republicans gained an advantage over the Democrats from 1980 forward. Culminating in 2005 and 2006, however, the Republicans were offering little more than nothing.

After the 2006 election, many a pundit argued that the Iraq War cost the Republicans the 2006 election. While it is true that the ongoing war did not help Republican Congressional candidates, it was not the central reason they lost.

You see, in politics, if you are not moving forward, it's easy to get knocked off your perch. When leaders are not cutting new paths and when they are not doing what it takes to stay ahead, they become subject to the vagaries of circumstances. Put another way, when someone is only treading water, even a small wave can overtake them.

In 2006, the Iraq War, Global Warming, and the Foley Congressional page scandal – none of those issues were so large as to cause the November defeats – especially (a) considering that the loss of American lives in Iraq (heartbreaking in any amount) is dwarfed by losses from prior major wars, (b) considering that Bush had a robust economy, (c) considering Bush had a great judicial record (as far as objective conservatives were concerned), and (d) considering the worthy foreign policy goal of defeating terrorism.

BUT. When a Party is perceived as doing nothing, the other Party, the Media and circumstances may well define that party - instead of that party defining itself. In other words, the Foley page scandal became a big story when Congressional Republicans had no compelling story of their own to tell or when the President failed to tell the one he had. So it can be no surprise that when voters came out of the booth to answer exit polls on November 7th, 2006, of course Iraq and Foley were the only questions to be asked. Why shouldn't it be? Republicans never gave them an alternate storyline.

Simply stated, the Republican Congress looked weak because it was not leading. Bush suffered because he allowed them not to lead and, in effect, he was not leading.

Combine that with Media distortions and the six-year itch and you have your recipe for mid-term losses – not huge losses (in 1994 the Democrats lost more) because the Democrats were still not offering anything – but losses nonetheless.

When all is said and done, by November of 2006, the Republicans forfeited their lead on ***Pillar Number One, Pro-Growth policies/reforms***. They had stopped acting like reformists and failed to pursue tax cuts. In response to the breach of the ongoing Contract with America, Republican voters were disenchanted. Independent voters were put off by the Iraq War especially in light of the lack of an alternative storyline - and the Democrats, despite offering no plan of their own, won back the Congress in 2006 by default.

The only question concerned voters had for Republican leaders in the wake of that election was whether they were aware of ***The Lessons We Should Have Learned.***

THE LESSONS WE SHOULD HAVE LEARNED

"I don't think much of a man who
is not wiser today than he was yesterday."
Abraham Lincoln

It is, of course, presumptuous for anyone to sit in judgment on the collective wisdom of millions of voters and attempt to bring order to their varied voices. Will and Ariel Durant, authors of *The Story of Civilization*, an eleven volume set, in their *Lessons of History*, asked writers of such ambition:

"Have you derived from history any illumination of our present condition, any guidance for our judgments and policies, any guards against the rebuffs of surprise or the vicissitudes of change?

Have you found such regularities in the sequence of past events that you can predict the future actions of mankind or the fate of states?

Is it possible that, after all, 'history has no sense,' that it teaches us nothing, and the immense past was only the weary rehearsal of the mistakes that the future is destined to make on a larger stage and scale?"

Comforted by the fact that the Durants proceeded to "compress a hundred centuries into a hundred pages of hazardous conclusions," it seems incumbent upon me to draw the few obvious conclusions from the past fifty years.

Lesson One: Pro-Growth Tax Cuts Work, Politically and Economically.

Lesson One, it seems, is the most important lesson of all and empirically, the easiest to prove. Nevertheless, it is surprising to see the number of Republican "leaders" who have yet to heed the lesson.

Lesson 1(A). Tax Cuts Work Politically. During the last 5 decades, only 3 Presidents could be said to be true champions of pro-growth policies: Kennedy (whose policies were enacted by Johnson), Reagan and Bush 43. All three followed Presidents that did not believe in such policies. All three achieved political realignments and/or political milestones – the other six Presidents did not.

Kennedy. As we have seen, Kennedy's policies helped the Democrats obtain huge majorities in both houses of Congress. In just ten years, the Democrats went from a minority party in Congress to huge majorities in both Houses: reaching highs of 68 – 32 seats in the Senate in the 1964 election and an astronomical lead of 295 seats to 140 seats in the House in that same election.

The difference in policies between the Kennedy and Eisenhower administrations on the major issues of the day, including but not limited to the three Pillars of *The New Conservative Paradigm*, were not so great so as to cause such a political realignment – except on the issue of the economy, i.e. taxes. The hallmark of their differences was the Kennedy cuts versus the Eisenhower caution. The Kennedy majorities would take two decades to even begin to reverse in earnest – and by who? The next President to champion his policies: President Ronald Reagan.

Reagan. The centerpiece of the Reagan Revolution was most certainly pro-growth tax cuts. Beyond the economic benefits, they engendered the "No New Taxes Pledge" - a policy pledge that has basically defined Presidential campaign politics ever since. Consider the following subsequent history:

- Reagan, the tax cutter, crushed Carter who allowed the tax burden to rise through bracket creep.

- Reagan wiped out Mondale who promised to raise taxes.

- Bush 41 defeated Dukakis, a life-long tax increaser, by promising "No New Taxes."

- Clinton defeated Bush 41 by promising tax cuts in the face of Bush 41's tax increases.

- Clinton raised taxes dramatically and even more dramatically the Congressional Republicans, who all voted against the tax increase, took back Congress for the first time in 40 years.

- Clinton defeated Dole despite Clinton's tax increases because Dole (who was against the Kennedy cuts) was known for voting for tax increases and refused to take the No New Taxes Pledge – meanwhile, Clinton campaigned anew for tax cuts.

- Bush 43 campaigned for tax cuts and defeated Gore who characterized tax cuts as a "risky scheme" and

- Bush 43, the proven tax cutter, defeated John Kerry who promised to raise taxes and Bush achieved increases in his Congressional majorities in three consecutive elections for the first time in many decades.

In other words, in seven out of the last seven Presidential elections, the winning candidate promised tax cuts. In those same seven elections, the candidate perceived as a tax increaser lost – except Clinton who lost the US Congress two years before but defeated Dole - another tax increaser.

Again, the reason why tax cutters tend to win since Reagan's time (beyond good economic results) is that the American electorate views that issue as a question of whether the candidate favors the needs of individuals and families (tax cuts) or whether candidates favor the needs of government (tax increases). For tax cuts advocates, it is the modern day equivalent of fighting city hall and it has enduring political power.

That is why it is difficult to *hazard* any other conclusion from the foregoing except the following: If you want to win the Presidency, campaign as a tax cutter. If you want to make a lasting political difference, champion large supply-side cuts. If you want to lose, the unquestioned route is to side with government and push for tax increases.

Why any Republican would suggest tax increases and thereby blur the lines between the Parties – especially since *tax cuts raise revenue and tax increases over time do not* - in the face of such empirical evidence is difficult to fathom. Nothing more need be said and, any Republican leader who fails to understand the foregoing, nay - who fails to trumpet the foregoing - is doomed to repeat history's mistakes.

While that may be the ultimate lesson for Republican leaders, it is up to everyday Republicans, activists and voters alike, to discourage any candidate who thinks otherwise.

Lesson 1(B). Tax Cuts Work Economically. If it was still was an open question as to whether tax cuts can boost an economy prior to Reagan, there can be little doubt of that now. As we have seen, once the bad effects of Carter's stagflation were wrung out of the economy, the Nation's economy grew at a 3.8% growth rate from 1983 to 1989. Between 1974 and 1981, the growth rate had been just 2.8%.[101]

We also know that twice before Reagan, Presidents gave Americans major marginal tax cuts and twice before the American Economy boomed: Kennedy/Johnson (a cut in the marginal rate tax rate from 91% to 71% resulting in 5.8% growth in 1964, and by 6.4% percent in 1965 and 1966) and

---

[101] Supply Tax Cuts and the Truth About the Reagan Economic Record, by William A. Niskanen and Stephen Moore, http://cato.org/pubs/pas/pa-261.html

the Harding-Coolidge tax cut (a cut in the marginal rate tax rate from 71% to 24%) that resulted in the Roaring Twenties, i.e. the economy grew by 59 percent between 1921 and 1929.[102] Although doubters still persist on the Left, the fact that robust economy activity occurred each time major rate cuts occurred - with no other significant common feature - places the issue beyond rational questioning.

Beyond the growth rate, the Reagan years also settled the question as to whether lower tax rates result in higher tax revenue. Total tax revenues climbed by **99.4** percent during the 1980s.[103] That followed a **62%** increase for Kennedy and **61%** increase during the 1920s.[104] These charts demonstrate the dramatic rise in tax revenues following those 3 major marginal rate tax cuts.[105] Seeing should amount to believing, especially for Republicans.

---

[102] The Historical Lessons of Lower Tax Rates by Daniel J. Mitchell, Ph.D. http://www.heritage.org/Research/Taxes/BG1086.cfm

[103] Same.

[104] Same.

[105] Charts from the Heritage Foundation.

THE NEW CONSERVATIVE PARADIGM

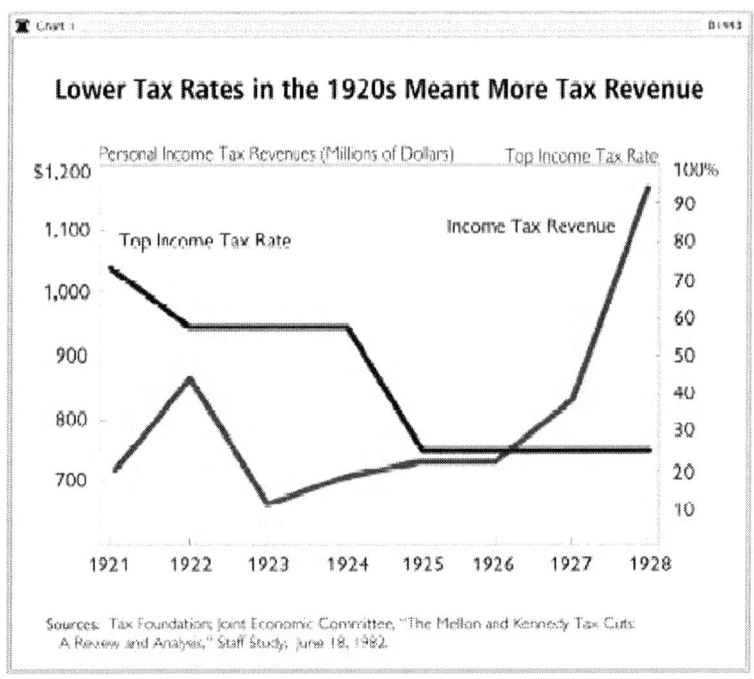

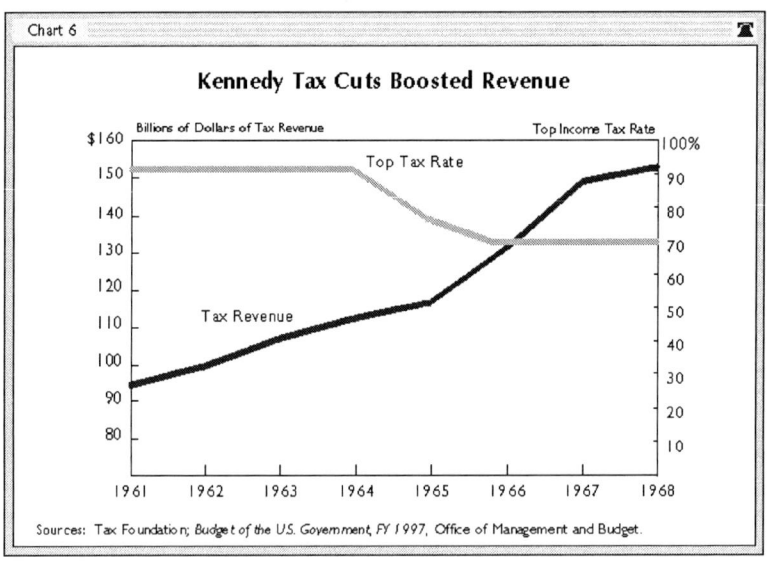

The Reagan Years

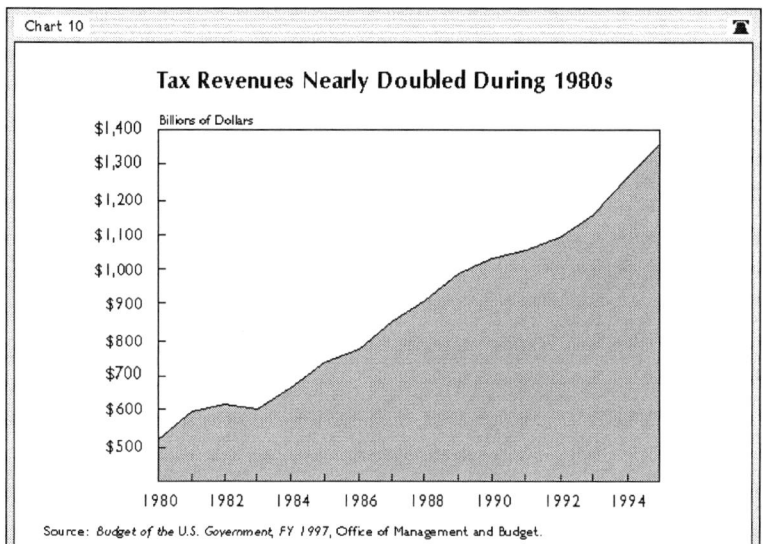

As for the Bush 43 cuts, beyond revenue growth in 2004 of 5%, the 15% in 2005 and similar rates in 2006 and 2007, consider the following:

"In the six quarters after Bush's tax cuts, real GDP expanded at a 4.6 percent annual rate, much faster than the 2.5 percent pace of the six earlier recovery quarters. Consumer spending jumped from 2.8 percent to 3.9 percent.

"Business investment in new plants and equipment surged to 13.4 percent from only one percent before the tax cuts. Personal income jumped to a five percent growth rate, nearly double the earlier speed of 2.6 percent.

"The average employment gain (combining both surveys) was 2.4 million compared with virtually no gain before the tax cuts. Corporate profits, without which businesses cannot create jobs, now stand at a record $1.118 trillion — 56 percent above their recession trough, 25 percent above the prior recovery peak of the late '90s, and at a near-record 9.5 percent of GDP.

"Broad stock market averages have jumped 60 percent from their lows. Home ownership is at an all-time high, as are existing home sales. U.S. household wealth stands at a record $51 trillion."[106]

As of July of 2007, tax revenues had increased $700 billion after the Bush tax cuts (the largest ever increase over a three-year span) and even the *New York Times* was required to admit revenue gains following the tax cuts as opposed to tax increases. Although the June 13, 2005 *Times* article called the "sharp increase" "unexpected," for Republicans it should be anything but unexpected. The experiences of Coolidge, Kennedy, Reagan and Bush should once and for all settle the question:

If you want to raise tax revenue, cut tax rates.

Lesson 1(C). Over Time, Tax Hikes Do Not Work Economically.

If History is clear that lower tax rates spur the economy resulting in higher tax revenues, it is also clear that the opposite occurs as well: If the government raises tax rates, in time, the government will receive less revenue over time

---

[106] Barreling Ahead into 2005, Larry Kudlow, National Review Online, http://www.nationalreview.com/kudlow/kudlow200412300923.asp

than if they had not raised taxes at all. Recall the 14th Century quote that "It should be known that at the beginning of the dynasty, taxation yields a large revenue from small assessments. At the end of the dynasty, taxation yields a small revenue from large assessments."

Need proof?

- In 1930, President Herbert Hoover raised the marginal tax rate from 25% to 63%. Roosevelt pushed them to 79% that same decade. [107] Although those tax hikes were not the only cause of the Great Depression or its length, they certainly contributed a great deal to both.

- In 1991, Republican Governor Pete Wilson's 1991 increased tax rates in California in response to a budget deficit. Years two and three of that increase resulted "in a revenue drop of $2 billion."[108]

- Income tax revenue grew slower under Clinton – and his tax hikes - than under Reagan and his tax

---

[107] The Historical Lessons of Lower Tax Rates by Daniel J. Mitchell, Ph.D. http://www.heritage.org/Research/Taxes/BG1086.cfm. Other contributing factors to the Great Depression included the Hawley-Smoot Tariff Act of 1930 that reduced trade and the Federal Government's decision to permit the money supply to shrink by nearly 1/3rd.

[108] California's Tax Follies, States can't tax their way back to prosperity, By Lawrence J. McQuillan and Andrew M. Gloger, published in National Review Online,

http://www.nationalreview.com/nrof_comment/comment-mcquillan040703.asp

cuts.[109] In other words, the Clinton tax hikes slowed the Reagan growth rates as did the Bush 41 hikes.

In a Picture Not Words

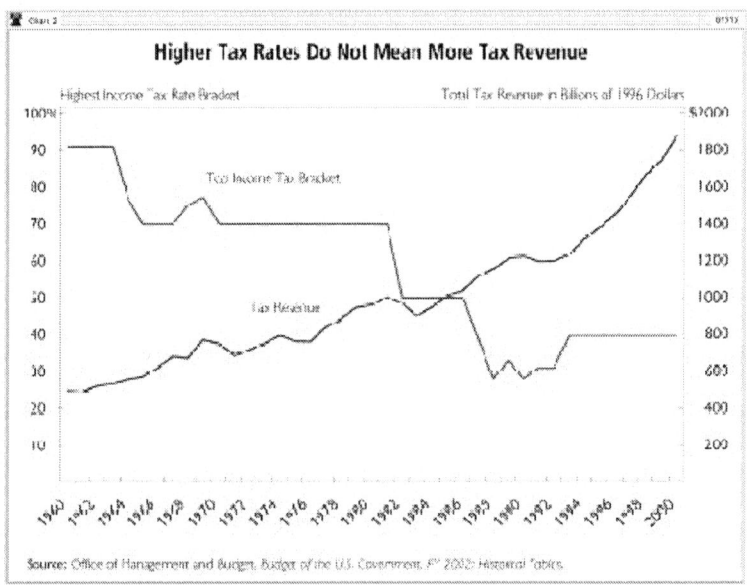

Disciples of Clinton and Robert Rubin are wont to claim that tax hikes resulted in balanced budgets in the later Clinton years. It is empirically correct that there were balanced budgets during some of the Clinton years. The tax hikes, in the short run, did net more tax revenues, but just like overfishing harms the fish population, the excess

---

[109] Are Supply-Siders All Washed Up? by Stephen Moore http://www.cato.org/dailys/6-06-97.html

Ruben/Clinton tax increases led to a recession starting in 2000. That tax hike-induced recession *negated prior revenue gains*. The relevant question, therefore, is not – in the short run, can higher tax rates raise tax revenue, but over time, do they do so in the aggregate? The answer is no, because they curtail future economic growth and lead to recessions which lead to lower tax revenues.

Lesson 1(D). Tax Hikes Do Not Work Politically.

At this point, it hardly seems debatable, but the fates of the Goldwater Republicans, the Mondale Democrats, the Dukakis Democrats, the Bush 41 Republicans, the Wilson California Republicans, and the Gore, Kerry and Daschle Democrats should be enough to convince even the most ardent – *Make tax increases your program and it is likely to be your last.*

Lesson 1 (E). The Name of the Game is Reform.

We have seen that the Democrats cornered the market on voters in the '60s by offering tax cuts for the haves and social programs for the have-nots. The modern day equivalent to such a strategy is offering tax cuts for the haves and government reform of underperforming programs for the have-nots.

Voters of the Internet age have become savvy enough and educated enough to know that the answer to every problem is not more money or a larger government program. Republican losses in the election of 2006, brought on by the big spending habits of Republicans, are a testament to that. Their objection to such Democrat solutions is not only that they are paying enough taxes already, but also that they understand Big Government has become less responsive to their local needs. In effect, they have bought Reagan's argument that "government is not the solution to our problem. Government is the problem," or perhaps Clinton's suggestion that the era of Big Government is over.

As the complexities of our times grow, there is no reason to believe that Reform won't be the name of the game in health care, education, and so many other issues.

Lesson Number Two: Big Political Gains Occur When Leaders Promote *The Three Pillars* and Inspire Their Country to Achieve Greatness.

Only three of the last ten Presidents had significant success and lasting effect on their Party's stature in Congress: Kennedy, Reagan & Bush 43 (pre-2006). All three had essentially the same program: Cut taxes, be strong on defense, believe in your country and its place and mission in the world and be respectful of its traditions – the Three Pillars of *The New Conservative Paradigm*. Nixon and

Clinton proved you can win without all three but Kennedy, Reagan and Bush 43 proved that championing all three can change the tide.

Kennedy, Reagan and Bush also engaged voters in a higher purpose. Kennedy asked his countrymen to help achieve:

"the kind of peace that makes life on earth worth living, the kind that enable men and nations to grow and to hope and to build a better life for their children -- not merely peace for Americans but peace for all men and women -- not merely peace in our time, but peace in all time."

Reagan believed that because "no arsenal, or no weapon in the arsenals of the world, is so formidable as the will and moral courage of free men and women" there would be a "'march of freedom and democracy" that would change the world.

For his part, Bush 43 cemented his place in History, during his 2005 second inaugural Speech, when he inspired so many as he told the world that:

"There is only one force of history that can break the reign of hatred and resentment, and expose the pretensions of tyrants, and reward the hopes of the decent and tolerant, and that is the force of human freedom.

"We are led, by events and common sense, to one conclusion: the survival of liberty in our land increasingly depends on the success of liberty in other lands.

The best hope for peace in our world is the expansion of freedom in all the world."

In reading those words from Kennedy, Reagan and Bush 43, ask yourself how far their inspirations are from Lincoln:

"In *giving* freedom to the *slave,* we *assure* freedom to the *free*—honorable alike in what we give, and what we preserve. We shall nobly save, or meanly lose, the last best, hope of earth."

or Washington:

"As Mankind becomes more liberal, they will be more apt to allow that all those who conduct themselves as worthy members of the community are equally entitled to the protections of civil government. *I hope ever to see America among the foremost nations of justice and liberality.*"

It is a lesson of our time, if not all times, that great leaders inspire their fellow citizens to achieve goals that transcend their times and their present day hardships.

In heeding that lesson, Kennedy produced huge majorities for the Democrats. Reagan changed Presidential politics and began the realignment which President Bush 43 enjoyed into 2005 by being the first President to win Congressional increases in three straight elections.

The power of **Pillar Number Two**, however, should not be overestimated. History has shown that, in the last forty years, the incumbent party does not fare well if they are prosecuting sustained foreign wars. Recall that Vietnam felled Democrat Lyndon Johnson. Republicans suffered the ill effects of the Iraq War in the 2006 mid-term elections – especially since they had no counter-balancing record of achievement. Political parties, therefore, should be wary of starting prolonged wars in favor of using overwhelming force and being able to secure the resultant peace. If they are caught in a long war, they best provide reform at home so that voters have an alternative storyline to follow other than the distortions of the Media.

Lesson Number Three: Trash Your Country, Its Ideals or Its Defense at Your Peril.

As we have seen, during the late 1960s, the Democrats were in some disarray. They were just four years removed from the huge 1964 Congressional victories. The Kennedy/Johnson tax cuts had produced unprecedented growth. Yet they managed to lose the 1968 election. Why? In part because Johnson was not the pro-growth advocate that Kennedy was. However, it was not as if the Republicans stole the issue from the Democrats. To the contrary, the Republicans were vocally against the Kennedy cuts. The Republican's 1968 Presidential candidate, Richard Nixon, did not repudiate those objections and certainly did not offer a tax cutting program of his own. Indeed, one year later he would raise tax rates on capital gains – an anti-growth measure. Thus, tax policy was not the determining factor of the 1968 election.

What changed, of course, was the view of America by the leaders of the Democrats. Their infighting over the Vietnam War left their party with a distinctly anti-American message which lost out to Nixon's Silent Majority. Thus, it can fairly be said, if the tax issue is neutralized by muddled voices, i.e. read the voices of Johnson, Nixon and Humphrey, Pillars two and three may be determinative.

The Democrats skepticism towards America and its purpose was a weakness carried over into the Carter years. It was instrumental in causing the loss of American prestige around the world as was demonstrated dramatically by the Iran hostage crisis. The Reagan victory was due, in part, to his rejection of such timidness which helped overcome the negative Media coverage of the Reagan tax cut proposals.

The rise of the effectiveness of the Christian Right, the Bible Belt and the Red States that so dominate the electoral map also present strong evidence that the modern voters value the Party that respects their values.

Even so, the Clinton years may well demonstrate the lesser role of **Pillars Two and Three** to **Pillar Number One**, pro-growth policies. We have already concluded that Bush 41 lost the 1992 election because he abandoned his no new tax pledge and Clinton was promising tax cuts. Clinton won that election even though the Democrats were still behind on **Pillars Two and Three** – although, it could be argued, that Clinton benefited from his Baptist ties in taking some Southern States from the less vocally spiritual Bush 41. By in large, however, the Democrats as a whole had not changed the dynamic.

Clinton won reelection despite raising taxes and despite the fact that Republicans stayed ahead on **Pillars Two and Three** and Clinton's high-profile troubles. Why? Because Bob Dole was not a credible surrogate on **Pillar Number One**, tax cuts. His was a muddled voice much more in the mold of Johnson, Nixon, Ford and Carter – none of whom had economic legacies. As a result, Dole was not able to convince the Country that he, a proven tax hiker, should replace another tax hiker, Clinton.[110] That factor was not helped by the fact that Dole did not come out for tax cuts until 2/3rds of the way into the campaign.

In sum, for purposes of our discussion, it remains evident that if the Parties are indistinguishable on the issue of taxes, depending on the circumstances, being behind on **Pillars Two and Three** can cost you a Presidential election, i.e. 1968, but it may not, i.e. 1996. It should be noted, however, that since 1996, the divide on **Pillar Number Three** has deepened and it may play a more determinative role in the

---

[110] It also did not help that Dole simply was not a man of obvious faith. As a result, Dole did not inspire the so-called Evangelical vote.

future if independents react adversely to ever more aggressive policies of the Left.

A Review of the Effect of Three Pillars in Modern Presidential History
The 1960 & 1964 National Elections

(Incumbent Party on the left hand side for all charts)

Pillars	Nixon (1960)	Kennedy		Johnson (1964)	Goldwater
No. 1 Pro-Growth		x		x	
No. 2 Defense	x	x		x	
No. 3 Family/ Traditions	x	x		x	x
Winner		Kennedy		Johnson	

In the 1960 and 1964 elections, the Democrats were recognized as strong or ahead on all three Pillars. Again, the difference between the Eisenhower Administration and the Kennedy Administration on foreign policy and traditional values was not dramatic. The difference on economic policy was significant because of three recessions under Eisenhower versus Kennedy's call for pro-growth policies. The result? A political re-alignment. The Republicans were behind on the tax issue in the first election and taxes and defense in the second. They lost both national elections and suffered politically in Congress for years to come.

The 1968 & 1972 National Elections

Pillars	Humphrey (1968)	Nixon	Nixon (1972)	McGovern
No. 1 Pro-Growth				
No. 2 Defense		x	x	
No. 3 Family/Traditions		x	x	
Winner		Nixon	Nixon	

In the 1968 and 1972 elections, neither Party espoused pro-growth policies. The Democrats, however, to their misfortune, turned vocally against America, its defense and its traditions. The anti-war, anti-traditional values Party lost both elections under those circumstances. However, in the absence of a leader on **Pillar Number One**, there was no political re-alignment in Congress or otherwise.

1976 National Election

Pillars	Ford (1976)	Carter
No. 1 Pro-Growth		
No. 2 Defense	x	
No. 3 Family/Traditions		x
Winner		Carter

The 1976 election was decided, of course, under the shadow of Watergate. It was also decided in an era where neither Party was particularly distinguishable domestically except that the Republicans were against the tax and spending excesses of the Democrat Congress but not against tax and spending. As such, the Republicans were the **"Me Too"** Party on taxes and spending and they had lost their lead on the family/tradition issue because of the scandals of the Nixon Administration and the perceived decency of Carter and his Baptist ties.

Ford nearly recovered from his decision to pardon Nixon to catch Carter at the end. But without an economic program, and in the relative calm of foreign affairs, the election was in all likelihood decided by something other than one of the three Pillars. It was decided in the aftermath of Watergate which produced a variant of **Pillar Number Three**. Certainly, no realignment there either.

1980 & 1984 National Elections

	Pillars	Carter (1980)	Reagan		Reagan (1984)	Mondale	
	No. 1 Pro-Growth		x		x		
	No. 2 Defense		X		x		
	No. 3 Family/ Traditions		X		x		
	Winner		Reagan		Reagan		

The 1980 and 1984 elections featured the first election since 1964 in which a **Party** held a strong position on all **Three Pillars**. The result? Reagan Democrats, the political realignment of voters and the beginning of a political realignment in Congress.

1988 & 1992 National Elections

	Pillars	Bush (1988)	Dukakis		Bush (1992)	Clinton	
	No. 1 Pro-Growth	?			No	?	
	No. 2 Defense	x			x		
	No. 3 Family/ Traditions	x			x	x	
	Winner	Bush				Clinton	

The 1988 election featured the first victory by a sitting Vice President since Martin Van Buren in 1836 – pure proof of the enduring Reagan re-alignment. Bush campaigned *promising* no new taxes. Fortunately for the elder Bush, who once used the phrase "voodoo economics" to describe

Reagan's pro-growth policies, he ran against a weak Democrat opponent on all issues in 1988. He would not be so lucky the second time around in 1992.

As we have seen, Bill Clinton was not about to repeat the mistakes of Carter, Mondale or Dukakis. Even though the elder Bush continued the Republicans' run on **Pillars Two and Three**, Clinton capitalized on Bush's default on **Pillar Number One**. Clinton campaigned for tax cuts and won despite trailing on **Pillar Number Two**. Southern Baptist ties minimized any Republican advantage on **Pillar Number Three**. In retrospect, the 1992 election is enduring evidence of the prominence voters place on **Pillar Number One**. In other words, it's the pro-growth policies stupid.

1996 National Election

Pillars	Clinton (1996)	Dole
No. 1 Pro-Growth		
No. 2 Defense		x
No. 3 Family/ Traditions		
Winner	Clinton	

The 1996 election should have been a no-brainer for Republicans. Clinton had forfeited the lead on the tax issue and the Republicans had taken back Congress. Nevertheless, this election appears to defy the charts and the Pillars.

The explanation lies in the fact that Clinton had the power of the incumbency, raised huge amounts of money and had the help of the ever more influential Major Media. The Republicans had the weakness of incumbency – that is not a reference to the Presidency. No, it was a reference to the fact that in the 1996 election the Republicans nominated their next in line – even though there was nothing compelling about his candidacy.

Far from compelling, Dole was a known tax hiker who refused to take the No New Tax Pledge. He was also not comfortable discussing the value of morality or religion. As such, he failed to motivate Republicans and values voters. The Democrats, meanwhile, mercilessly defined Dole prior to Dole receiving matching funds in the late summer.

One can only wonder the fate of the 1996 election if the next-in-line for Republicans had been Jack Kemp.

2000 & 2004 National Elections

Pillars	Gore (2000)	Bush		Bush (2004)	Kerry
No. 1 Pro-Growth		X		x	
No. 2 Defense		X		x	
No. 3 Family/ Traditions		X		x	
Winner		Bush		Bush	

The 2000 and 2004 elections were similar to the 1980 and 1984 Reagan elections. The Republicans, perhaps learning from the Bush 41 debacle and the Clinton/Dole loss, nominated a pro-growth candidate and proceeded to win two elections in a row. Bettering that, they won three consecutive national elections when you consider their Congressional gains in 2002.

Have You Noticed the Critical Lesson?

As you review the charts, there is one critical lesson to be gained. There is not a single election in which a Presidential Candidate lost when that candidate was *convincingly* ahead on the issue of taxes, i.e. who was for the individual and families, versus the champion of government – not one. That is perhaps the enduring lesson of *The New Conservative Paradigm*.

Leading up to 2008, however, some Republican leaders appear to be ready to repeat 1968 – to blow an uncertain trumpet on the three Pillars as they jockey for position in the Presidential sweepstakes. The question remains, will they have learned the lessons of Kennedy, Reagan and Bush 43? Or was the past a "weary rehearsal of the mistakes" that they are destined to make on a larger stage and scale?

As of this writing it is difficult to say for sure. But many *New Conservatives* appear most unlikely to let them do so without a fight.

LESSONS IN ACTION

"Insanity: doing the same thing over and over again and expecting different results."
Albert Einstein

If Einstein is right, and there are few grounds on which to dispute his point, then presumably an equally true corollary would be Political Insanity: ***refusing to do what works***. Perhaps the other side of that coin is the saying that "Those who do not learn from history are doomed to repeat it."[111] The simple question for the Republican Party, in the coming decade, will be whether it relies on what worked in the past or whether it will voluntarily walk away from the lead it has by ignoring the past.

As we shall see, the decade of 2010 and beyond will present an enormous fiscal challenge for our Country. If the Republican Party is to regain its Majority Party status in Congress, it will have to renew a critical aspect of the Reagan Revolution or risk minority status.

Before we look at the decade ahead, however, we would do well to remember the historical dynamic that governments do not start out *large and efficient* and wind up *small and inefficient*. Quite to the contrary, the history of governments, including our own, is that they start out small and decentralized and relatively responsive to the governed. Since power abhors a vacuum and therefore loves to centralize, governments tend to grow and grow until they reach the point of being more large and inefficient than actually helping the governed.

---

[111] First said by Spanish-born American philosopher George Santayana (1863 – 1952) and repeated by President Harry Truman.

Indeed, our own colonies needed to be coaxed into being a Nation. In reaction to their experience with the British Monarchy, the Colonists drafted a decentralized Articles of Confederation. They were agreed to by Congress on November 15, 1777 (after 16 months of debate) but not ratified and in force until March 1, 1781 - nearly three and one-half years later. Not centralizing enough to hold the Nation together or protect it, they were then replaced in 1789 by the ratification of the Constitution – all told, a 12 year process. Centralization, however, did not stop there.

Perhaps the easiest way to understand the centralization dynamic is through the lens of the federal budget. In 1821, the federal budget was but $15 million dollars. One hundred years later, just before the Great Depression, the federal government expenditures were now $2.92 billion – and then, we were off to the races:[112]

1925	2.92 billion
1930	3.32
1935	6.4
1940	9.47
1945	92.71 (WWII)
1950	42.56
1955	68.44
1960	92.19
1965	188.23
1970	195.65
1975	332.33

---

[112] All figures are gross dollar amounts not adjusted for inflation.

1980	590.95
1985	946.39
1990	1,252.53 trillion
1995	1,519.13
2000	1,788.83
2005	2,479.4
2006	2,600
2007	2,969

The chart starts just before the Great Depression because it is a good point of reference for what lies ahead. Prior to the Great Depression, there were no New Deals and the federal government was comparatively small. In response to the serious crisis, a crisis badly exacerbated by government, the societal reaction was not to fall back on days of self-reliance or even to blame government - but, instead, to look for an even larger governmental solution to the problem – a pattern familiar to all of history. With that, the federal government began a process of swift growth that continues to accelerate.

The growth in the last 25 years alone is stunning. In the 1970s, in gross terms, spending tripled. It tripled again by 1995 and has nearly doubled since then. Today, the federal government spends nearly $20 of every $100 spent each day. By 2075, if we stay on our current path, the federal government will spend at least $40 out of every $100. Long before 2075, however, the US will be confronted with a challenge which could be larger than the Great Depression.

The Triple Witching Decade

In stock trading, the Triple Witching hour occurs four times a year when stock options, stock-index options, and stock-index futures all simultaneously expire. Markets can often be *volatile* during that hour as investors cash out. For the US, the Triple Witching Decade will be 2010 to 2020 – if not before. If we are not careful, our investors may well cash out. It will be the Triple Witching Decade because during that decade:

1. the US Public/Private Pension Crisis will be at full tilt (if not before then);
2. Social Security will be under water; and
3. the Medicare Crisis (state and federal) will be front and center.

The breadth of this book is certainly not sufficient to cover those coming crises, but a short reflection is required to place the magnitude of those issues in context.

The US' Private Pension Crisis.

According to the federal Pension Benefit Guarantee Corporation (PBGC), the government agency charged with guaranteeing pension benefits for employees of *private* sector companies that fail, as of 2005, "defined benefit pension plans in the U.S. have promised $450 billion more in benefits than they have in assets."[113] Worse than that: "a new Government Accountability Office (GAO) report that details the level of underfunding in the 100 largest defined benefit pension plans between 1995 and 2002 shows that underfunding is getting worse."[114] For example, at one point in 2004, at least 14 companies that comprise the S&P 500 owe their workers more in pension payments than what the whole company would be worth in liquidation.[115]

At this time, the US taxpayer does not pay for the bailouts of such unfunded pensions. Annual per-employee premiums pay for the "insurance." However, if a severe shortfall in the program occurred, "a taxpayer bailout of the agency is inevitable."[116] It may well be inevitable because the history of our Country, at least since the 1930s, is that in times of economic crisis, the "solution" is ever larger government. Witness the Savings & Loan bailout during the late 1980s and early 1990s which cost taxpayers somewhere

---

[113] Are Pensions the Next Fiscal Crisis? by David C. John, Tim Kane, Ph.D., and Rea S. Hederman, Jr., The Heritage Foundation, WebMemo #756, June 2005,
http://www.heritage.org/Research/SocialSecurity/wm756.cfm

[114] Ibid.

[115] http://www.forbes.com/personalfinance/estate_planning/2004/08/12/cz_bc_0812pensions.html

[116] Are Pensions the Next Fiscal Crisis? by David C. John, Tim Kane, Ph.D., and Rea S. Hederman, Jr., The Heritage Foundation, WebMemo #756, June 2005,
http://www.heritage.org/Research/SocialSecurity/wm756.cfm

over $150 billion dollars.[117] It is no stretch to assume that may happen again, with respect to the private pension crisis, and only the most naïve would believe that the pressure on Congress for such action would be anything less than monumental. The private pension crisis, however, is just the tip of the iceberg.

The Public Pension/Medicare/Social Security Crisis

The coming (if not already arrived) Pension/Medicare/Social Security crisis will dwarf the private pension crisis. According to some, the

"long-term economic health of the United States is threatened by $53 trillion in government debts and liabilities that start to come due in four years when baby boomers begin to retire. . . . The $53 trillion is what federal, state and local governments need immediately — stashed away, earning interest, beyond the $3 trillion in taxes collected last year — to repay debts and honor future benefits promised under Medicare, Social Security and government pensions. And like an unpaid credit card balance accumulating interest, the problem grows by more than $1 trillion every year that action to pay down the debt is delayed."[118]

---

[117] The Cost of the Savings and Loan Crisis: Truth and Consequences by Timothy Curry and Lynn Shibut, http://www.fdic.gov/bank/analytical/banking/2000dec/brv13n2_2.pdf

[118] The looming national benefit crisis, By Dennis Cauchon and John Waggoner, USA TODAY, http://www.usatoday.com/news/nation/2004-10-03-debt-cover_x.htm

Somewhere between 2011 and 2015, Medicare will arguably be "bankrupt." I say arguably because few believe the "government" won't bail it out. In 2017, if not before, Social Security starts taking in less than it pays out. That means that politicians will no longer have the so-called Social Security surplus to bail out their other expenditures. By 2020, the combined Medicare/Social Security deficit will exceed $200 billion per year.

At this point, it is worth reviewing again the chart from the introduction of this book – and asking the question, can all of this continue indefinitely?

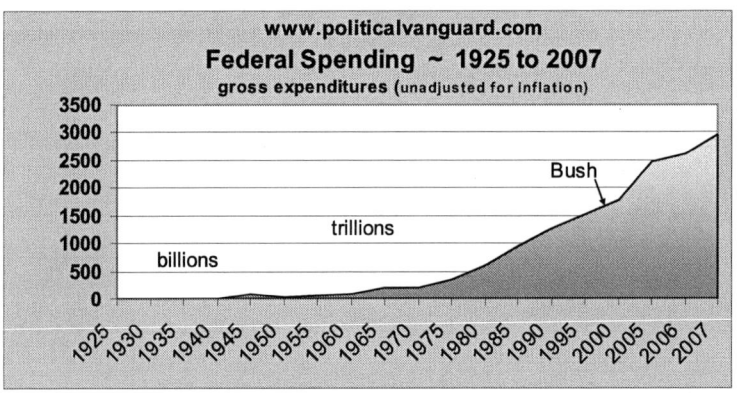

Can federal spending really continue to grow that fast without a total collapse of the system? Keep in mind that federal spending jumped over 8.5% in 2005 under a Republican Congress and a Republican President and that the "new Medicare prescription drug benefit, [enacted under a Republican Congress and a Republican President]

increased the government's unfunded obligations by $8.1 trillion over the next 75 years." [119]

Worse yet, "there is no budgetary consideration of the actual financial commitments resulting from policy changes enacted by Congress because they are paid well into the future."[120] In other words, Congress spends with barely any consideration for future costs – all that matters is the budget for the current year. Want to enact a new spending entitlement? No problem, we have the money now. The future be damned.

The problems of health care and public pensions, however, are not confined to the federal government. In California, the State's pension liability is said to exceed $63 billion – or more than half its 2007 budget. The California State Teachers' Retirement System is facing a $24 billion deficit. In the San Francisco Bay Area, Contra Costa County is facing unfunded liabilities in excess of $2.5 billion (which is over twice its annual budget) while Los Angeles County's pension shortfall is over $5 billion.

Why Something Needs to Be Done

---

[119] Time for the Federal Budget Process to Include Unfunded Entitlement Obligations, by Alison Acosta Fraser, The Heritage Foundation, http://www.heritage.org/Research/Budget/bg1818.cfm

[120] Ibid.

The point of this Chapter is not to be an alarmist – although alarms should have gone off by now, if not well before now. The point is to have the reader understand that the next ten years could present the US with a challenge no less in size than the Great Depression or World War II. Unless we act as a Nation to get government under control, we are headed for a fiscal meltdown. That meltdown would result in a significantly lower standard of living for all Americans.

Of course, it is likely that the leaders of the Left will be of little help in this crisis. They will claim that the Republicans are abandoning the poor by advocating reduced government. In other words, they will demagogue these issues endlessly.

It should be obvious though, that we do a much larger disservice to those on the government dole by failing to address these issues now and thereby courting a future meltdown that could leave the poor with little to no services and no savings on which to fall back. Beyond that, the likely economic breakdown will leave them without jobs as well. Thus, to not get government under control will amount to abandoning the poor - not the opposite. Put another way, a bankrupt government is not a compassionate government.

So, what to do? Simply stated, we must act now and not wait for the storm to come ashore. As we consider what action to take, it must be noted that, contrary to Thoreau's admonition that "things don't change, we change," ***things have changed and so have we.***

Things changed in that government has already grown out of control. Prior to World War II and the Great Depression, our federal government was still relatively small. It had room to grow. Now however, we don't have the option of 60 years of new, explosive, government growth. In that same time, we have changed. Most are tired of growth in government and endless taxes – many are ***Silent No More.***

All of which begs the question, that since the federal government spends nearly $20 of every $100 spent each day, does anyone really think Americans will stand idly by as we march toward 2075 when the federal government will spend at least $40 out of every $100? Will Americans accept payroll taxes of 25%, such as in France, in addition to ever higher income and sales tax rates, to pay for these programs? Could we even reach such a point? Sadly, the answer is yes. But . . . it is not inevitable.

A Menu of Needed Reforms

At all times we need to remember that government is a man made institution. It is an ***un***natural disaster waiting to happen when it grows to such proportions. Quite frankly, Ronald Reagan would say in the face of the current spending crisis that:

"The crisis we face is not the result of any failure of the American spirit; it is failure of our leaders to establish rational *goals* and give our people something to order their lives by."

As far as inevitability, Reagan said and would say again:

"I do not believe in a fate that will fall on us no matter what we do. I do believe in a fate that will fall on us if we do nothing."

Thus, we can fairly conclude that doing nothing is not an option. We need to get about the business of establishing rational goals to reining in the unsustainable growth in government before it hurts nearly everyone and helps a diminishing few.

One last dose of reality, however, as we start this process. Sadly, and obviously, we cannot always or even often count on the leaders of either Party to do the right thing by controlling spending. It is an unfortunate truism that once elected, politicians, who otherwise knew government must be controlled, too often become overwhelmed by *Edifice Complex* – a psychological affliction that seems to require them to justify their political existence (1) by appropriating ever greater amounts of money to government programs, and/or (2) by having something built, i.e. a bridge, a building, etc., to which they can claim credit.

President Calvin Coolidge alluded to this affliction years ago when he stated:

" Nothing is easier than the expenditure of public money. It doesn't appear to belong to anyone. The temptation is overwhelming to bestow it on somebody."

Given the magnitude of pork barreling, by both Democrats and Republicans, over the many years since Coolidge made that remark (when the Federal budget was under $3 billion – today it is $3 trillion), it seems logical to conclude that there is no known cure for the *Edifice Complex*.

In the absence of that cure, quite frankly, it will be up to the *Silent No More* to lead our leaders out of this crisis. In other words, *We the People* must undertake a series of measures to reduce the opportunities for politicians to act out their spending urges.

The following is a list of reforms by which *We the People* can undertake to do just that. The list is not meant to be exhaustive. Nor is the list an attack on any individual program. Instead, they are measures designed to (a) reform the programs we already have, and (b) change the structural components of modern government that permit the unsustainable, unlimited growth we face today.

In doing so, those reforms will not hurt the poor as the leaders of the Left will claim. They are common sense attempts to stop politicians from forcing our government over the edge and hurting the poor even more.

1. **<u>Enact True Part Time Legislatures</u>**. There is no immutable law of physics which requires full-time legislatures. They are the favorite of politicians - not average Americans. Worse yet, full-time legislatures violate President James Madison's desire for a citizen legislature that would retire to their normal jobs so as to reflect the common values of our citizens instead of the professional class the legislators have become. Furthermore, every day any legislature is in business is another day spending goes up not to mention tax rates and fees. A part-time legislature reduces those temptations by as much as half. So, if you want to slow down spending, simply stated, give politicians less opportunity to do so, i.e. less days to tax and spend. Therefore, state legislatures should only be in session for four to five months out of the year. If they fail to pass a budget within that time, then the budget should revert to the expenditures of the prior year and the legislators' pay should be reduced for failing to do their job.

2. **<u>Enact Two Year Budget Cycles</u>**. Simply stated, the federal and state governments should be required to budget two years at a time (such as Texas does), not the

one-year cycle most use now. That set-up offers the added benefit of requiring longer term planning._ More importantly, two-year budget cycles have a similar effect to that of a part time legislature. They reduce the opportunity of legislators to spend money in half again because, barring a super majority vote for a state crisis or a special session on a particular issue, budget items would be considered only once every two years. Combined with a part-time legislature, politicians would only have four to five months every two years to tax and spend compared to the 18 months most take advantage of now.

3. **Enact Real Budget Spending Limits**. Government growth, at least at the state level, should be restricted roughly to the growth in population and the CPI increase. Without budget caps, legislators from all Parties legislate with blank checks and credit cards with no limits. We must take away those blank checks and cancel those credit cards. In their stead, we should enact real budget caps. Colorado has an effective statute and, no surprise; it was one of the few states that did not have a fiscal crisis as a result of the Clinton-9/11 recession.

4. **Require Accrual Based Government Accounting**. Quite frankly, the reason politicians spend

without regard to the future is because there is no real consideration of future spending. Why? Well, in part, because government uses the "Cash Basis" method of accounting. "Cash-basis budgeting does not recognize the true costs of operating the federal government . . . Accrual accounting [on the other hand] is widely recognized as providing information that is superior to cash-basis recordkeeping and is used in business precisely because it forces [its users] to recognize and plan for future obligations."[121] In other words, each spending program would require its true long-term cost be carried on the federal books (unlike now), i.e. there would be long-term planning and accounting. Since cash basis accounting does not – it has to go. Once voters see how poorly their politicians have managed their future, they may think twice about voting for incumbents that are irresponsible.

5. **<u>Require Costs-Benefit-Analyses for all Programs.</u>** Most government programs are enacted without a cost-benefit analysis. In other words, programs are enacted without a serious review of whether they will actually work. Moreover, funding for programs goes on

---

[121] Time for the Federal Budget Process to Include Unfunded Entitlement Obligations, by Alison Acosta Fraser, The Heritage Foundation, http://www.heritage.org/Research/Budget/bg1818.cfm

and on without a rational determination as to whether the program is helping the needy – or whether the needy still exist for the program in question. Periodic cost-benefit analyses of programs can lead to realistic determination of whether future programs make sense and whether existing programs should be modified to help their intended beneficiaries or whether they are still needed. That can result in better government and the reduction of wasteful spending.

6. **Require Zero Based Funding**. Most governments determine next year's budget by adding on to last year's budget. Rarely is a considered analysis done of whether the prior funding met its goals, i.e. helping the needy. Further, given the mandates tied to most funding, i.e. restrictions as to exactly where money can be spent, wasteful funding can go on and on without real oversight. Requiring zero based funding will force legislators to review how your money is spent every year and will require them to justify each program – which takes time and reduces their ability to create new programs. That too can lead to better government.

7. **Sunset Government Programs**. Most government programs are enacted and never end – regardless of whether they are helping their intended

beneficiary in the manner that was originally contemplated. If programs were sunsetted, i.e. terminated at a future date certain, before that date arrives, needed programs could be addressed with an eye to the problem as it exists at the time they are reconsidered - not as it did years before. In that way, outdated programs and taxes could be phased out in favor of other priorities like Medicare.

8. **Governments Must Move to Defined *Contribution* Programs and Away from Defined *Benefit* Programs**. It is the wont of politicians to guarantee an outcome to government pension beneficiaries. Unfortunately, "defined benefit" pension programs, as they are known, guarantee retirees a fixed amount each year such as their last year's salary. That results in massive unfunded liabilities for government pensions and social services because it has the affect of keeping retirees on the payroll for life. "Under the switch [to defined contribution programs], employees and employers (the government) would both contribute to an individual investment account. Upon retirement, the size of each public employee's pension would depend on the contributions made (including the employer match) and the personalized investment strategy the employee used. This way, the State could still offer attractive

retirement plans but lawmakers couldn't make promises they can't pay for."[122]

9. **Government Employee Pension Benefit Increases Should Require Voter Approval**. Any pension benefit must be voted on by taxpayers. You are paying the freight and therefore you should directly vote on whether there should be an increase in government pensions. Politicians have proven that they cannot be trusted with this issue. San Francisco County voters have this power and San Francisco programs are fully funded. That is so because in order get any pension increase, proponents have to demonstrate a balanced budget to the voters. Meanwhile, neighboring Contra Costa County, which does not send such increases to the voters, has a $2.5 billion funding deficit.

10. **Outsourcing Non-Essential Services**. The simple truth is that we cannot afford to pay for all of the government programs that are already on the books. Therefore, the question becomes: Do we care more about services being provided or who provides those services?

---

[122] *How to Keep Pension Promises on the Road to Solvency* by George Passantino http://www.rppi.org/pensionpromises.shtml

Obviously, the answer is the former, and therefore government at all levels must stop looking to be the provider of all services associated with government. For instance, it is not essential for government to be in the janitorial business. By doing so, however, the burden on taxpayers is higher because government must foot the bill for the retirement of all those employees as well as other costs associated with being an employer. Those costs, and countless others like them, could be reduced by outsourcing non-essential services thereby freeing up money in favor of other priorities like Medicare.

Those are just a few ideas for helping to bring governments back from the brink of bankruptcy. All of those Reforms can be enacted by **We The People** through the initiative process. In states such as Colorado, California and others, reform movements utilizing the initiative process are already underway – sometimes without the support of politicians. The remainder of the Country needs to join their revolution and place our so-called leaders on notice that spending without consequences will in fact have consequences for them.

A Game Plan for Republicans

The coming crisis will not only challenge our Nation, but also test whether the Republican Party can be the

Majority Party in Congress. Whether it will be the Majority Party will depend, of course, on whether it deserves that status.

As the coming spending crisis unfolds, the following "givens" must be kept in mind:

- It is more than likely that the Democrat leaders will simply demand new taxes and higher spending;
- The Party of *No* is historically the minority Party,
- Therefore, as pensions, Medicare, Social Security and other large government programs reach critical funding junctures in the years just ahead, Republicans cannot simply say *No* – No to programs and No to voters. Nor can they campaign simply by saying we need budget cuts - lest they become the Party of *No* versus the Party of handouts – the Democrats.

So the dilemma for the Republican Party is how it stays the Party of *Yes* during a budgetary crisis when spending must be reduced from the projected levels. The answer is by doing what works: (1) Stay firm on tax cuts because they produce greater revenues over time and (2) embrace Reform.

Beyond lower taxes, the "Yes" Republicans must provide real reform designed to maximize taxpayers' resources not bureaucracies coffers. Reagan began the modern era of reform from the moment he was elected. It was successful. Given the problems ahead, it would be insanity not to follow his lead.

By championing the reform movement, the Republican Party will be offering the average voter something positive: better government and lower taxes. The Democrats, for their part, will fight reform at every turn and as a result: (a) will be the party of the status quo, i.e. big government, and (b) the *Party of NO* – no to Reform. Thus, the dynamic is in place for the Republicans to successfully champion the issue of Reform and thereby be the Majority Party nationally.

The Power of Yes

Keep in mind that one of the great successes of President Reagan was his ability to change the national mood. He was optimistic and America became so. Psychology 101 will teach you that people respond to positive images, actions and especially leadership. Positive agendas and positive leadership lead to majority status because, when it comes to voting, generally, voters like to vote *for* something more than they like to vote *against* something.

Therefore, the game plan for the Republican Party is simple: give them something to vote for and keep the

Democrats on the defensive. Year after year, the Republican Party and its leaders, state and federal, should put forth combinations of reform initiatives and legislative agendas driven by reforms. In that way, Republicans can not only control the agenda – but give voters a reason to vote for them.

It is a winning, positive formula that should be replicated around the Country again and again. Given that 2010 is just around the corner, there is no sense waiting for the fiscal storm to come ashore. Republicans should act now, seize the higher ground, control the agenda of tomorrow. In doing so, it can once again become the Majority Party nationally.

FINAL THOUGHTS HOPES

"Visualize this thing that you want, see it,
feel it, believe in it.
Make your mental blue print, and begin to build."
Robert Collier

We have nearly reached the end of our journey. Along the way, we have heard from the great Leaders in American History: Washington, Lincoln, Kennedy & Reagan to name a few. Not surprisingly, they share an ability to inspire but not just to inspire. Each summoned their fellow citizens to **Higher Purposes**. Under each of them, Americans achieved more than could be anticipated under difficult circumstances. Certainly, that is one definition of Leadership.

Amidst our review of history, we have discovered that our government is growing out of control with spending that has more than doubled in the previous ten years. We wonder whether any one person can govern this Country or some of its States. We have also learned, however, that we are not speaking just about 2007. Indeed, the same held true for 1980. Spending rose dramatically in the 1970s at a time when the Cold War dragged on seemingly without an end in sight. Pundits wondered whether the Presidency could be managed by just one person.

At the time, a leader came along – a true leader. His words are worth reading again:

"We're not, as some would have us believe, doomed to an inevitable decline. I do not believe in a fate that will fall on us no matter what we do. I do believe in a fate that will fall on us if we do nothing."

Amidst such uncertainty, he suggested that:

"The crisis we face is not the result of any failure of the American spirit; it is failure of our leaders to establish rational *goals* and give our people something to order their lives by."

The issues Ronald Reagan faced in the early 1980s are not much different than the issues we face today. Back then, neither the Democrat leaders nor government had answers to the malaise fostered by Jimmy Carter and the policies of our government during the preceding years.

Reagan had those answers and for a time he changed the course of government.

He was well aware the government-made problems of inflation, slow growth and rising taxes were robbing Americans not just of their wealth but of their spirit as well. So, in the face of government growth that was out of control, he willed the Congress to reduce spending. He recognized that government was not the solution to our problems but, instead, that government was the problem - and so he set about reforming government through regulatory reform. And, of course, he cut taxes because doing so was the economic equivalent of setting people free.

Those rational goals can serve our Nation once again. Within the next few years, along with the explosive growth of government, we will face a growing pension crisis, a growing immigration problem and a government that has no answers to the everyday problems of everyday Americans.

Quite frankly, the current crop of Democrat leaders seem to have no answers to those problems because their twin mantra of raising taxes and ever larger spending are no longer viable answers for a country that is overtaxed and treasuries that are overdrawn. The answer is Reform and the Republican Party can be and must be its champion.

We can take comfort in knowing that the path upon which we must walk is well worn with the Wisdom of Reagan. We should understand the issues facing America call for answers that Republicans have and the Democrat leaders do not. And so, with Reagan's example in mind, Republican leaders have the opportunity to reject inevitable decline and they have the opportunity to set rational goals.

Those goals must once again affirm the Three Pillars of *The New Conservative Paradigm*. Our Presidential and Congressional candidates and leaders must once again adopt a powerful agenda that preserves our freedom and simultaneously lifts our spirits. They cannot simply believe in the economic effects of tax cuts. They must passionately understand the nexus between tax cuts, freedom, inspiration and hope.

They must also understand that we are not interested in electing managers of our government. We want leaders that will change the course of government. Beyond that understanding they need to communicate that passion to the American people and let them know once and for all that they understand that they represent **We the People** not government.

As grassroots activists, we must demand no less from our leaders and we must remind them at every turn that tax cuts and reform led the way to the Republican Majority in Congress – not spending, not tax increases.

The task we set out to achieve this time may well be difficult. Surely though, we cannot believe that the task we face compares with the task Lincoln faced on the morning of his inauguration as a President facing Civil War. It was Lincoln's principles and his resolve that led the way.

Lincoln's **Optimism** was essential as well and as we have seen, it is a trait shared by all great leaders. So we too must have that optimism and we must know that civilizations, like individuals, must always be looking ahead. So we cannot "think of today's failures, but of the success that may come tomorrow."[123]

If we do, we shall be able to carry on the legacy of Ronald Reagan and we shall have it in our power to "begin again."

---

[123] Helen Keller

ACKNOWLEDGEMENTS

We are, in many respects, who we were – as a person, as families and even civilizations. In that light, I must thank all those family members, friends, teachers who helped weave the fabric of my life. They have brought me to today . . .

Chief among them are my parents. During the time I wrote this book, my Mother fell quite ill with cancer and overcame it as she has previously. She unquestionably is the strongest person I have ever known. Everyday she lives her life for her beliefs. This book is a small effort to honor her courage and her life . . . Incredibly, my Father fell ill with the same type of cancer as this book neared publication. Along with my Mother, he taught me that honesty, intellectual and otherwise, is more important than success. This book tells the truths as I now know them and with the skills that his strength and honesty have forged.

My parents also blessed me with seven brothers and sisters – all of whom, Edward, David, Mark, Mary, Diane, Lisa and Nicole, have kept me on my toes through the years. We certainly all don't agree on the issues, but their intellectual vibrancy certainly nurtures mine. My sister Nicole deserves a special mention for her help researching this book and her work as an Editor of Politicalvanguard.com.

As for my friends, I wish to thank the following for their kindness and encouragement:

Bruce and Valerie Schooley for some time encouraged me to write a book and so here it is! They have supported my political endeavors at every turn including helping me with this book. I can't thank them enough.

Stephen Frank has been a great friend and supporter of mine as well. He spent many an hour reading the early transcripts of this book as well as my many other writings. Thank you again and again for all of your help.

Darcy Linn, thanks for all the work you have done not only for Politicalvanguard.com but also in reading the early transcripts of this book. Neither would have been possible without your help.

Gretchen Medel, thank you for all the work you do to making my political endeavors easier and successful including reading the early transcripts of this book.

Greg Poulos – who has a Masters in US History – thanks for reading this book so closely and making sure the trees and the forest were kept in proper perspective.

Patricia Welch – thanks so very much for your help on my CRP work without which I could not spend the hours needed on this book.

Melanie Morgan of KSFO who helped me at the very beginning to have my voice be heard.

Brian Sussman of KSFO who has extended a helping hand to me while asking for nothing in return and who encourages me at every turn and to Inga Barks of KMJ and KERN who also has been so very kind enough to let my voice be heard.

To the many volunteers around the state of California who continue to fight for the Reagan Revolution every day and who have shown many me so many kindnesses and inspire me including the great volunteers of the Republican Party of Contra Costa, the California Republican Party and my many friends in my favorite of organizations: the California Federation of Republican Women.

Finally, to my daughter Juliana from whom I learn everyday and whose love keeps me going.

PUBLISHER'S NOTE

As the first major release from TMK Books, it has been an absolute honor to work with Tom Del Beccaro. As a former politico, I can't imagine how Tom found the time to write this book, keep his immense speaking schedule, and be a great father, friend, online magazine publisher, and juggle sleep – all at the same time. His ideas are definitely fresh – taking the successes of the past and translating them for the future of the Republican brand as he sees it.

I would like to thank Tom for taking the leap of faith with me, as we break new ground. He is quite possibly the most energetic person I have ever met. He truly is a force of nature. Look out, Democrats. This book is the playbook for beating Hillary Rodham Clinton in 2008. Or any Democrat who underestimates the power of freedom. It is also a powerful message to Republicans that might stray from solid economics and turn to "voodoo" for a magic bullet on Election Day.

As the Publisher at TMK Books, it is important the voices we share are diverse. I believe America will be strengthened by building cultural and literary bridges across the globe. We are the real countries… it is up to every free person to contribute, participate, and embrace our fellow human beings. The future is up to us.

--- *Elizabeth Blackney*